The Brumback Library

IN MEMORY OF:

Mrs. Doris Ayres

PRESENTED BY:

Mr. & Mrs. John J. Carr
& Son

GOOD · OLD · DAYS®

Favorite Songs
of the
Good
Old Days™

Hillside Serenade by McClelland Barclay © 1928 SEPS: Licensed by Curtis Publishing

Edited by Ken and Janice Tate

HOUSE of
WHITE
BIRCHES
PUBLISHERS
SINCE 1947

Favorite Songs in the Good Old Days™

BD MB CP DA RC MW

Editors: Ken and Janice Tate
Managing Editor: Barb Sprunger
Editorial Assistant: Joanne Neuenschwander
Copy Editors: Michelle Beck, Nicki Lehman, Läna Schurb
Assistant Editors: Marla Freeman, Marj Morgan, June Sprunger

Publishing Services Manager: Brenda Gallmeyer
Graphic Arts Supervisor: Ronda Bechinski
Cover Design/Production Artist: Erin Augsburger
Traffic Coordinator: Sandra Beres
Production Assistant: Jessica Tate
Photography: Tammy Christian, Christena Green, Kelly Heydinger
Photography Stylist: Tammy Nussbaum

Chief Executive Officer: John Robinson
Publishing Director: David McKee
Marketing Director: Shirrel Rhoades
Book Marketing Director: Craig Scott
Editorial Director: Vivian Rothe

Printed in the United States of America
First Printing: 2004
Library of Congress Number: 2003105325
ISBN: 1-59217-034-X
Good Old Days Customer Service: (800) 829-5865

1 2 3 4 5 6 7 8 9

Dear Friends of the Good Old Days,

Songs have been my lifelong friends. They accompanied me through my childhood and past the rocky years of adolescence. They helped me express my love and provided solace in times of grief. If I was in a silly mood, there was a song to express it; if there was a time of deep spiritual reflection, a song framed it in my mind.

Caroling by Charles Berger, House of White Birches Nostalgia Archives

When I think of our favorite songs back in the Good Old Days, three specific memories flood to my mind.

The first was just before Christmas when I was 5 or 6 years of age. My Uncle B.H., Daddy's youngest brother, was visiting and brought his guitar to accompany us for carols. After a few songs, B.H. asked me to sing *Silent Night* alone. Later I overheard him tell Mama and Daddy, "You know, Kenny has a really good voice."

That was the first time I remember hearing anyone say I was good at anything, unless it was getting into mischief. I don't know if it was real or imagined, but it seemed that Mama looked on me with a bit more pride after that. At family music parties Daddy asked me to sing as he and his brothers played guitars, fiddles and mandolins. That simple song and compliment gave me the confidence to take on the world, now that I was good at something.

Then there was singing with my sister as we did the dishes. My brother was five years older than I, so he ended up with all the "boy" chores until I got a bit older. My sister and I accompanied suds, washrags and towels with hearty renditions of *K-K-K-Katy* and *Please Shine Down on Me*: "Oh, Mister Moon, Moon, bright and silv'ry moon, won't you please shine down on me?"

It was at that sink that we developed a bond that has stood the test of time and distance. There is nothing like the memory of sharing work and song together to keep you close. Yes, I know we could have had the normal brother-sister relationship without the nightly serenade at the sink, but I don't know we would have had the same depth of love without it.

Finally, I think about an old friend, Gary, whom I met at church. Gary was a fine Christian man, but had had a rough early life. He had served in the Navy and had worked in Alaska for years, and he had the vocabulary to prove it. Once he told me that he still was overcoming the use of "cuss" words. "So now, whenever I think I'm gonna cuss about something," he confided, "I start singing a hymn."

A few months after that conversation, we were working on a widow's house. Gary was nailing down a piece of corrugated steel roofing out of sight from where I was working. Bang! Bang! Bang! His hammer rang out on the metal roofing. Then—thud! I knew that hammer had met flesh.

Gary yelped in agony, and I was ready for my ears to turn blue. "You dirty …!" There was a painful pause. Then, with voice quavering slightly, I heard Gary begin: "Then sings my soul, my Savior God to Thee: How great Thou art!"

That's when I realized the real power of our favorite songs. Whether it was giving us confidence, sealing sibling love or helping us overcome swearing—songs helped us become something new, something better.

Janice and I hope you enjoy these memories of how some of those favorite songs helped us become who we are today. We hope you are reminded of all the childhood ditties, toe-tapping dance tunes, love serenades and church hymns that became your Favorite Songs of the Good Old Days.

Ken Tate

✤ Contents ✤

Old Favorites • 6

Sunrise Serenade ....
When I Wished Upon a Star ....
Alice Blue Gown ....
Mom Was a Singer ....
Mother Sang the Old Songs ....
Springtime in the Rockies ....
Red River Valley ....
The Magic of Singing ....
Rock Me to Sleep ....
A Special Day, A Special Song ....

Songs of Love • 34

Our Love Song Was *My Happiness* ....
Yankee Rose ....
Remembering Nelson Eddy ....
Let Me Call You Sweetheart ....
Remembering Lilli Marlene ....
Peg O' My Heart ....
Tying the Leaves ....
When Your Old Wedding Ring Was New ....

Faith & Inspiration • 56

Grandpa Dodd and *The Old Rugged Cross* ....
Mother's Favorite Hymn ....
Is My Light Shining? ....
O Holy Night ....
Live in the Sunshine! ....
My Brother's Mistake ....
Life's Railway ....
A Song of Faith & Hope ....
Where We'll Never Grow Old ....

Just for Fun • 80

Take Me Out to the Ball Game ....
Rudolph's Rise to Fame ....

Yust Going Nuts!..88
Monkey Business 90
Roll Out the Barrel..92
The Bus Ride 94
Round the Mountain 98

n Our Youth • 100

Outside of You..102
Two Wrongs and a Right 105
Getting Our Kicks 106
Heart Tugger..110
Johnny's Song..112
Good Night, Sweetheart.......................................113
Christmas in Any Language 114

Home & the Old Folks • 116

God Will Take Care of You 119
Silver Threads and the Broken Heart 120
My Nostalgic Song 124
Blest Be the Tie That Binds...................................126
Mother Was a Lady 129
A Song From the Old Country 132
Love & the Power of Music 134
Danny Boy...135
My Mother's Voice 136
Old Folks at Home 139
The Story of a Song 140

ove of Country • 142

It's a Grand Old Flag 144
Three Cheers for the Red, White & Blue.................146
A Beloved Anthem...148
Music Under the Stars..150
The Other Side of the Fence..................................152
America the Beautiful 156
Index 159

OPERATIC EDITION
Hiawatha's Melody of Love
Song
Lyric by
Alfred Bryan &
Artie Mehlinger
Music by
Geo. W. Meyer
Frederick S. Manning
6
Jerome H. Remick & Co.
NEW YORK

Old Favorites

Chapter One

If you are like me, many of your old favorites are tied to the long-ago days of your youth. Those songs remind us of those carefree days of adolescence and beyond.

Two of my old favorites both have a Native American theme. My Great-Grandmother Blevins was a Cherokee who died in Oklahoma Indian Territory. Though I never knew her, stories of her life always intrigued and inspired me.

As a strapping young boy, whenever my comrades and I played cowboys and Indians, my Cherokee blood always pushed me to choose to be an Indian. I romanticized about living on the plains, hunting buffalo and deer with my lance and bow and arrow. If I must die, whether in the hunt or in the battle, I determined that I would die heroically.

One of my favorites from those days was the wonderful ballad *Red Wing* (words by Thurland Chattaway, music by Kerry Mills). In it, the Indian maid Red Wing pines for her braves, who had died in battle:

Red Wing

There once lived an Indian maid,
A shy little prairie maid,
Who sang a lay, a love song gay,
As on the plain she'd while away the day;
She loved a warrior bold,
This shy little maid of old,
But brave and gay,
He rode one day to battle far away.

She watched for him day and night,
She kept all the campfires bright,
And under the sky, each night she would lie,
And dream about his coming by and by;
But when all the braves returned,
The heart of Red Wing yearned,
For far, far away, her warrior gay,
Fell bravely in the fray.

Now, the moon shines tonight on pretty Red Wing,
The breeze is sighing, the night bird's crying,
For afar 'neath his star her brave is sleeping,
While Red Wing's weeping her heart away.

Like Tom Sawyer imagining his aunt and Becky mourning his death, I could see my loved ones weeping over my grave and exclaiming, "So young! So brave!"

After I was old enough to leave cowboy-and-Indian games behind, my romanticized view of death began to change to a romantic view of what I had to live for! I began to look for a Red Wing of my own (although my Red Wing became a redhead named Janice).

With the first strains of love on heartstrings, *Red Wing* took a back seat to *Hiawatha's Melody of Love*. The title, of course, reminded me of Longfellow's famous epic poem. The words of the chorus reminded me that even warriors love:

Hiawatha's Melody of Love

And the song they sang was Hiawatha's melody.
Just a golden memory
Of the days that used to be.
As they sat entranced beneath
the weeping willow tree
Ev'ry leaf up above
Seemed to tremble with love.
And the evening breeze sang Hiawatha's melody.
Sang it sweet and tenderly
Like a love's rosary.
Now the songbirds in Spring
Still remember and sing
Hiawatha's melody of love.

The cover painting on the sheet music wistfully told me that perhaps some Red Wing out there was looking for me, her Hiawatha.

Maybe *Red Wing* or *Hiawatha's Melody of Love* was a favorite of yours, too. I'll bet one of these memories of melodies from days gone by will remind you of your Old Favorites.

—Ken Tate

Sunrise Serenade

By Doretha Dillard Shipman

When I see the title, play the tune or hear the big bands strike the first note of *Sunrise Serenade,* my thoughts begin to whirl. I am faced with memories of my youth, World War II, my sweetheart in the Air Corps and my family—mom, dad, sister and brother.

After I married and had my family of seven children, the words began to mean even more to me. They never fail to bring back treasured thoughts of the past. The tears flow sometimes when I think of my mother, father, sister and husband deceased, the children married and me living alone. But I still feel comfort whenever I play and sing *Sunrise Serenade* in my sentimental, thoughtful moods.

World War II was the main concern of the time. Daddy listened intently to Walter Winchel telling the news and C.C. Williford forecasting the weather over the battery-run radio. But when Saturday night rolled around, it was a must to hear the Hit Parade with the big-band sound. *Sunrise Serenade* was among the top ten songs in the nation, and we loved that song. I think Mother enjoyed it as much as we three children did, because I was never denied the privilege of sitting down at the piano to try my luck at playing it. My notion to perform sometimes struck at dishwashing time. Anyone who has washed dishes on a hot summer day with the dishpan sitting on a wood-burning stove to keep the water hot would realize that Mother must have loved that song—and me—to let me get out of washing dishes in order to play it.

We had lived through the Depression, which was now giving over to wartime. Jobs had been scarce, but now workers were sought for wartime duties. More money was in circulation and people could afford to buy things like radio batteries, if they were not rationed. This was a big plus for us; communication and recreation depended on the radio.

As the 1940s passed, my sister started her job at an ammunition plant, the Arkansas Ordnance Plant in Jacksonville, Ark., and my brother was beginning his preaching service. I was still in high school and was finishing my credits in three years in order to go work for the War Service as soon as I turned 18. Our families were parting, and I was sad about that. When we got together, which was still often, we enjoyed being together, but regretted when it was time to go our separate ways again. But before we parted, we always ended our wonderful time together with the beautiful melody of *Sunrise Serenade.* This became a tradition for us.

During wartime, our little country community missed the many families who had gone to other states to work. I missed the young folks with whom I had grown up, but when I began to feel sad, I took a trip down memory lane and played our old tunes. With a touch of the piano, the notes and songs of our yesterdays made life brighter.

I was 18 in September. I went to work, and on Dec. 27, 1943, I married the schoolmate and soldier of my dreams. After he served more than three years in the Air Corps, World War II ended and he came home. We started our own little family on a little farm in the Ozark Mountains.

I missed the old player piano at Mom and Dad's. It was impossible to own one, as we were furnishing our first real home with the bare necessities. However, on Sundays, after church, we gathered at their home. And when it was time to say our good-byes, we ended a nearly perfect day with *Sunrise Serenade.*

My sister found the first piano I ever owned. Once it was in our home, things began to feel more like the Good Old Days, and I took time to play the old pop songs. I'm sure you can guess what was included.

As my family grew, I didn't have much time for daytime serenading. I spent my time tending to children, washing on a scrub board, gardening, haying and helping to run a dairy farm. Although life was busy, it was happy, and the meaning of my favorite song began to register in my mind as its words corresponded with our daily lifestyle. "Good morning, good morning, you sleepy head," it began—and you can bet that I needed just a few more minutes of sleep!

Then it continued, "Get out of that bed, though the air is soft as silk, it's time to get your morning's milk, come on, wake up, get up!" We did get up, and built the fire in the wood-burning cookstove. Bacon, hog jowl or ham and eggs with milk gravy and homemade country biscuits and coffee were prepared. I always had it ready, steaming hot, when my husband came back from getting our "morning's milk," as the song said. It was truly a good morning.

Now, as I sing the chorus, I think back to the country life we shared and enjoyed. "Look at the grass, silver in the sun, heavy with dew." My husband was always looking for the first blades of grass. He called it "the green cast." This meant the cows were sure to enjoy good grazing, which meant more milk and less spent on the feed bill.

"Look at the buds, you can almost see how they're breaking through." How great it was

after a long, hard winter to see the first signs of spring. The buds were swelling, birds singing to their mates and gently dropping food into their babies' mouths. *Sunrise Serenade* didn't leave the birds out—"Look at the birds feeding all their young in the sycamore, but you better get on with your morning chores! Just take a look at the new-mown hay and the sugarcane." This phrase is filled with many precious memories, for we loved to go into the hay field with the children and eat a picnic lunch near the cool spring. Before returning to the field, a quick, cooling dip in Buffalo River or Water Creek was sheer joy and a must for the children.

Finally comes the finish of a lovely day: "Looks tonight there should be a moon down in lovers' lane—There you go daydreaming, when it's time that you obey that sunrise serenade!"

Many nights, after the busy day was done and the children were in bed, I sat down at the piano and played those old songs the children still love and ask for. One daughter sings them professionally and tells her audience, "Mother used to play us to sleep with those tunes."

With a good night to all, my wish is for you to awake to a beautiful sunrise and a happy serenade to keep in your heart the whole day long. ❖

Sunrise Serenade

Words by Jack Lawrence
Music by Frankie Carle

Good mornin',
Good mornin',
You sleepyhead,
It's dawnin',
Stop yawnin',
Get out of that bed …
Say, the air is soft as silk,
It's time to get the mornin' milk,
Come on!
Wake up!
Get up!
Look at the grass
Silver in the sun,
Heavy with the dew.
Look at the buds;
You can almost see

How they're breakin' through.
Look at the birds
Feedin' all their young
In the sycamores.
But you better get on
With your mornin' chores.
Just take a breath
Of that new-mown hay
And the sugarcane.
Looks like tonight
There should be a moon
Down in lovers' lane—
There you go daydreaming
When it's time that you obeyed
That sunrise serenade!

Over the Garden Wall

Words by Harry Hunter
Music by G.D. Fox

Oh, my love stood under a walnut tree,
Over the garden wall …
She whisper'd and said she'd be true to me,
Over the garden wall …
She'd beautiful eyes, and beautiful hair,
She was not very tall, so she stood on a chair,
And many a time have I kissed her there,
Over the garden wall.

Chorus:
Over the garden wall,
The sweetest girl of all,
There never were yet such eyes of jet,
And you may bet I'll never forget
The night our lips in kisses met,
Over the garden wall.

But her father stamped, and her father raved,
Over the garden wall,
And like an old madman he behaved,
Over the garden wall.
She made a bouquet of roses red,
But immediately I popped up my head;
He gave me a bucket of water instead,
Over the garden wall.

One day I jumped down on the other side,
Over the garden wall,
And bravely she promised to be my bride,
Over the garden wall;
But she scream'd in a fright, "Here's Father,
    quick,
I have an impression he's bringing a brick!"
But I got the impression of one good kick,
Over the garden wall.

But where there's a will, there's always a way,
Over the garden wall,
There's always a night as well as a day,
Over the garden wall,
We hadn't much money, but weddings are
    cheap,
So while the old fellow was snoring asleep,
With her lad and a ladder she managed to creep
Over the garden wall.

Young Love by Jay Killian, House of White Birches nostalgia archives

When I Wished Upon a Star

By Helen Colwell Oakley

One of my favorite songs down through the years has been *When You Wish Upon a Star.*

As a young girl growing up on the farm out Pierce Creek way, in Binghamton, N.Y., the beautiful words impressed me. I can't remember them exactly, but they promised, "When you wish upon a star, makes no difference who you are, your dreams will come true!" I believe this to be true, for I believe we were all created equal and stand a chance of finding happiness. I attended a little country school at first and city schools later. My classmates included people of many different kinds—Jews, Poles, Slavs, black, white—and I loved them all regardless of who they were or where they had come from.

When You Wish Upon a Star was an inspiration for me, for it expressed hope for all of us. It encouraged us to reach for the stars and believe that anything is possible if your heart is set upon it. Perhaps that is why I had a happy childhood on the farm during the Great Depression, for I seemed to accept the hard times and make the best of them by finding enjoyment in everyday happenings. When folks hear that I was on the farm during the Great Depression, I'm often asked if it wasn't dreadfully hard. But I always reply "No." In fact, I had a happy childhood.

I sometimes have been looked down upon for coming from a farm, or for not having as much money as others have, but this never bothered me. I always believed that I was as good as anyone, especially when I remembered the words of the song: "Makes no difference who you are." I never lost faith that my dreams would come true, and I have always liked folks for their pleasing personalities and good deeds, rather than their class or status in life. I would advise people to listen to the words of that song, for it inspires people to have faith in themselves and realize that all things are possible.

When You Wish Upon a Star taught me some lessons about keeping my chin up and loving folks no matter who they are. I enjoyed many moments of pleasure listening to this lovely song on the radio. I find that many of today's songs seem difficult to understand. I prefer the oldies, including this favorite, which tells a story and entertains. ❖

When You Wish Upon a Star

Words by Ned Washington
Music by Leigh Harline

When you wish upon a star,
Makes no difference who you are;
Anything your heart desires
Will come to you.

If your heart is in your dream,
No request is too extreme
When you wish upon a star
As dreamers do.

Fate is kind;
She brings to those who love
The sweet fulfillment of
Their secret longing.

Like a bolt out of the blue
Fate steps in and sees you through.
When you wish upon a star
Your dreams come true!

Alice Blue Gown

By John Dinan

Like most moms, my mother hummed and sang tunes that had been popular during her teenage days. Although none of those songs lasted in popularity from her generation to the next, I can recall a few of them.

When my memory bell is rung by some tune or lyric, I remember some of the words to *You Are My Sunshine*, *Hear the Wind Blow*, *The Red River Valley* and several others. These were simple tunes with clearly coherent lyrics: "You make me happy when skies are gray. You'll never know, dear, how much I love you. Please don't take my sunshine away." Sweet and simple.

My mother sang another tune that I could never figure out: *Alice Blue Gown*. I never asked my mother what this song was all about, and I never would have known, had it not been for the research done by Stacy A. Condery of Monmouth College, Monmouth, Ill.

While Ms. Condery doesn't mention the tune specifically, she does write some interesting lines concerning Teddy Roosevelt's daughter, Alice. "Alice," she says, "took the country by storm." She was a wild one, who played poker with men, smoked in public, and pulled pranks usually associated with the male gender, such as releasing a snake into the midst of a garden party, jumping fully clothed into a swimming pool, etc. She was a regular at the racetrack and did other things only men were expected to do at the time.

Ms. Condery goes on to write: "Alice Roosevelt became an overnight sensation after her 1902 debut." Babies were named after her, and "capital dressmakers touted 'Alice blue' as the fashionable color of the day."

Reading this brought me back to the 1930s, when I listened to my mother sing *Alice Blue Gown*—and a light went on for the first time. My mother sang while she did the dishes and other household chores, and I remember the tune to this day.

Alice Roosevelt went on to complete foreign tours as an American goodwill ambassador and was quite popular worldwide. Her presence in Europe and Asia left Teddy (rather than Alice, whom the press dubbed "Princess Alice") alone on the front pages of American newspapers.

This quote is attributed to Teddy: "I can be president of the United States or I can govern Alice. I cannot possibly do both."

I wonder if my mother knew the story behind Alice Blue Gown? ❖

Alice Blue Gown

Words by Joseph McCartney
Music by Harry Tierney (1919)

I once had a gown—it was almost new,
Oh, the daintiest thing,
It was sweet Alice blue;
With little forget-me-nots
Placed here and there,
When I had it on,
I walked on air,
And it wore, and it wore, and it wore,
Till it went and it wasn't no more.

Chorus:
In my sweet little Alice blue gown,
When I first wandered down into town,
I was both proud and shy,
As I felt ev'ry eye.
But in ev'ry shop window

I'd primp, passing by;
Then in manner of fashion, I'd frown
And the world seem'd to smile all around.
Till it wilted I wore it,
I'll always adore it,
My sweet little Alice blue gown.

The little silkworms
That made silk for that gown,
Just made that much silk
And then crawled in the ground,
For there never was any thing like it before,
And I don't dare to hope
There will be anymore,
But it's gone 'cause it just had to be,
Still it wears in my memory.

I'll Take You Home Again, Kathleen

Words and music by Thomas P. Westendorf

I'll take you home again, Kathleen,
Across the ocean wild and wide,
To where your heart has ever been,
Since first you were my bonny bride.
The roses all have left your cheek,
I've watched them fade away and die;
Your voice is sad whene'er you speak,
And tears bedim your loving eyes.

Chorus:
Oh! I will take you back, Kathleen,
To where your heart will feel no pain.
And when the fields are fresh
　　and green,
I'll take you to your home again.

I know you love me, Kathleen, dear,
Your heart was ever fond and true;
I always feel when you are near,
That life holds nothing dear
　　but you.
The smiles that once you gave
　　to me,
I scarcely ever see them now,
Tho' many, many times I see
A dark'ning shadow on
　　your brow.

Repeat Chorus

To that dear home beyond
　　the sea,
My Kathleen shall again return,
And when thy old friends welcome thee,
Thy loving heart will cease to yearn.
Where laughs the little silver stream,
Beside your mother's humble cot,
And brightest rays of sunshine gleam,
There all your grief will be forgot.

Repeat Chorus

Mom Was a Singer

By Charley Sampsell

Mom was a singer. Only a few of her many friends in our farm community in southwestern Michigan were aware of her vocal prowess. She never sang solos or duets in public, but she always engaged with enthusiasm in the hymn singing at services of the West Mendon Evangelical Church and at Grange and other meetings.

Every morning, as she fired up our big, black, iron-and-chrome wood-burning cookstove, she started her day with a song. And except for frequent periods of conversation with Dad and me or other family and friends, she continued to sing until bedtime.

Her repertoire was extensive and varied. As a high school girl, she had lived with her aunt and uncle who owned the hotel in Mendon, Mich. With her cousin, who later became a professional musician and bandleader, she attended many Chautauqua shows, concerts and other musical events. She soon developed an interest in and familiarity with all the secular music of the early 1900s.

After high school and before she married Dad in 1913, Mom found religion and regularly attended church services of several denominations. Her vocabulary of hymns and sacred music soon surpassed her popular portfolio.

By the time I was born in 1924, Mom could light the stove in the morning with a cheery version of *Red Wing,* go to the henhouse and gather a dozen fresh eggs with *The Old Rugged Cross,* start the bacon frying while singing *Moonlight Bay* and belt out *Rock of Ages* while washing the dishes.

I often wondered why she didn't perform some of those songs I liked so well in public. Her voice seemed very pleasant to me and she surely had no trouble carrying the tunes. I also wondered how she could sing all day long without repeating the same song. But there was an exception to that rule. I could count on hearing *The Church in the Wildwood* several times each day. It was Mom's favorite.

Throughout my grade school years, she continued her daily concerts, adding an occasional new tune that Little Jack Little, Singing Sam the Barbasol Man or Kate Smith sang on the radio. By the time I left home to live with relatives and attend high school, I had assimilated a substantial portion of her mental file of music. But I soon realized that while I had the melodies down pat, I was a little sketchy on the words. Most of the choruses were solid, but the verses demanded considerable effort for adequate recall. Nevertheless, the words and melodies acquired in those long-ago days were indelibly etched into my memory.

I realized many years later that I awake each morning with a different song in my mind. Often it is one of Mom's hymns, or a song I learned elsewhere during my youth. It may also be one that arrives from no identifiable source and for no apparent reason. Whatever its origin, my morning song persists with me for several hours, and I find myself whistling or humming the tune as I repeatedly run the words through my mental verse reader. I still enjoy the exercise and view it as part of the pleasure of awakening each morning.

> *By the time I was born in 1924, Mom could light the stove in the morning with a cheery version of* **Red Wing***, go to the henhouse and gather a dozen fresh eggs with* **The Old Rugged Cross***, start the bacon frying while singing* **Moonlight Bay***, and belt out* **Rock of Ages** *while washing the dishes.*

When, as a 13-year-old boy, I was away from Mom, Dad and home for the first time, I was overwhelmed by homesickness. Oh, how I wished I could again awaken in the morning to hear Mom singing, "There's a church in the valley by the wildwood"!

As the months and years dragged by, school vacations were too short a reprieve from my loneliness and too brief a chance to return to the welcome security and warmth of our family. I did enjoy playing trombone in the high school band and occasionally getting a chance to play for dances. My own mental portfolio of tunes began to expand.

When World War II came along, I was once again far from home and missing my family and Mom's cheering presence as much as ever. Three years later, as I rode the Twilight Limited train home from the Air Corps separation center, I was elated to return to our little farm and Mom's welcome voice. I felt I was definitely in the running for the "Happiest Passenger On Board" award.

In 1984, I was 60 years old. Mom was 97 and living in a nursing home where she shared a room with her closest friend, Linna. On my last visit to them, we enjoyed an hour together in the day room of the nursing home. Linna was still able to play the piano and Mom sang along as best she could. When Linna surged into *The Church in the Wildwood,* Mom's voice became suddenly stronger and the words clearer: "No spot is so dear to my childhood as the little brown church in the vale." I decided it was my favorite song, too. ❖

The Church In the Wildwood

Words and music by Dr. William S. Pitts

There's a church in the valley by the
    wildwood,
'Tis the loveliest place in the dale;
No spot is so dear to my childhood
As the little brown church in the vale.

Chorus:
Oh, come, come, come, come …
Come to the church by the wildwood,
Oh, come to the church in the dale;
No spot is so dear to my childhood
As the little brown church in the vale.

How sweet, on a clear Sabbath morning
To list' to the clear-ringing bell;
Its tones so sweetly are calling,
"Oh, come to the church in the vale."

There, close by the church in the valley,
Lies one that I loved so well;
She sleeps, sweetly sleeps, 'neath
    the willow;
Disturb not her rest in the vale.

There, close by the side of that loved one,
'Neath the tree where the wildflowers
    bloom,
When farewell hymns shall be chanted,
I shall rest by her side in the tomb.

Mother Sang the Old Songs

By Dorothy Behringer

Mother sang those old songs,
Like *Rock of Ages, Cleft for Me*,
When things in life would trouble her,
She'd sing, sweet songs of Thee.

And *Blest Be the Tie That Binds*
She'd sing from dawn to dusk, you see,
No matter what her chore would be,
Those songs, to my heart, would touch.

Or when some trial came so abrupt,
With answers she could not see,
You'd hear her so heavenly sing,
Oh, Jesus Savior, Pilot Me.

Remembering her in her rocking chair,
With a baby at her breast,
My mother, so warm and lovely,
To me was so heavenly blest.

Fragments of tunes you'd hear her sing,
Whenever she was alone,
"Be it ever so humble," came clearly,
"There's just no place like home."

She's gone now and my thoughts return,
To me, fond memories cling,
Bouquets of tunes I once had heard,
From old songs my mother sang.

By the Light
Of the Silvery Moon

Words by Ed Madden
Music by Gus Edwards

Place park, scene dark,
Silv'ry moon is shinin' through the trees;
Cast two, me you,
Sound of kisses floating on the breeze;
Act one, begun
Dialogue: "Where would you like to
    spoon?"
My cue, with you,
Underneath the silv'ry moon.

Chorus:
By the light of the silvery moon
I want to spoon
To my honey I'll croon love's tune
Honey moon, keep a-shining in June
Your silv'ry beams will bring love
    dreams
We'll be cuddling soon
By the silvery moon.

Act two, scene new,
Roses blooming all around the place;
Cast three, you me,
Preacher with a solemn looking face.
Choir sings, bell rings
Preacher: "You are wed forever
    more."
Act two all through,
Ev'ry night the same encore.

Repeat Chorus

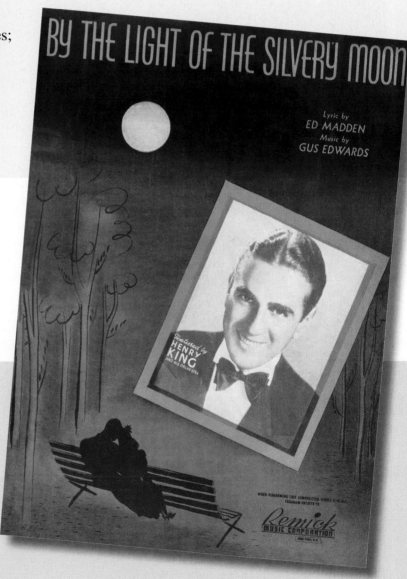

Hiking in the Mountains by John Clymer © 1952 SEPS: Licensed by Curtis Publishing

Springtime In the Rockies

By Dorothy Carter Steiner

*M*ama stood at the wood cookstove in our farm kitchen, stirring the gravy and humming along with her favorite tune, *When It's Springtime in the Rockies*. Behind her, we three little girls stood with our elbows on the old wooden table and our chins in our hands, listening intently.

"Now, don't wind it too tight!" Mama always cautioned us.

We had to be supervised to play the precious phonograph she had placed carefully in the center of the table. That phonograph was in a black carrying case. An expanding file in the lid held 12 thick, round records.

Each record had an RCA Victor label with a picture of a dog and a big Victrola horn. The turntable played one record at a time. We had to handle those records gently and set the arm with the needle lightly on the right ridge where the music began. We had to take care not to scrape the needle across the grooves or forever after that there was a scratchy click with every revolution. The music sounded tinny and there was no volume control, but who knew the difference?

A little round metal container with a hinged lid was fastened near the turntable and contained several extra needles. In time, the needles got dull, but Mama solved that problem by sharpening them on a piece of fine sandpaper before inserting a needle in the playing arm. In the middle of the 1930s Depression, one certainly did not fritter money away on new phonograph needles. Nor did we buy new records. So we played the ones we had over and over. Mama had worked in the city during the 1920s, and she had saved her money to buy that phonograph. I am so glad she did!

We never tired of that music. Like Mama, I especially liked *When It's Springtime in the Rockies*. Maybe it was the calming, smooth rhythm. We lived in northern Minnesota, so we were nowhere near the mystical Rocky Mountains, but maybe I liked the song because I loved the springtime with the birds arriving and new wildflowers hiding under the leaves, waiting to be found. And spring brought refreshing rains instead of the troublesome snowstorms that sometimes isolated us.

In those days when it seemed that all Mama and Daddy ever did was work on our little farm, that music added a different perspective to our lives. It appeared to have a healing effect; at least, it stopped our sibling squabbling for a while.

There was one song that we kids simply could not stand. But in fairness, we always played that one too, because we played all the records in order. Since then I have learned to appreciate that particular song.

Indeed we were careful with the windup crank on the side of the machine, which had to be turned to wind the spring before we could play another record. We knew that if we broke the phonograph, that would be the end of music in our house, for we had no radio or musical instruments except for a little harmonica that Mama sometimes played for us.

Mama sang along with the music when we played the phonograph. Daddy liked music, too, but he couldn't sing and he refused to dance. Even so, Mama sometime persuaded him to take us all to the Saturday-night dances at the schoolhouse when local musicians tuned up their violins and mandolins. Aside from singing in school and Sunday school, that was the only other time we heard music.

Our one-room school did have a pump organ, but one of its pedals was broken. Nobody knew how to play it anyway. So that phonograph was truly a blessing. *When It's Springtime in the Rockies* was an exhilarating and refreshing song. ❖

When It's Springtime in the Rockies

Words by Mary Hale Woolsey
Music by Robert Sauer

The twilight shadows deepen in the night, dear,
The city lights are gleaming o'er the snow,
I sit alone beside the cheery fire, dear,
I'm dreaming dreams from out the long ago,
I fancy it is springtime in the mountains,
The flowers with their colors are aflame,
And ev'ry day I hear you softly saying,
"I'll wait until the springtime comes again."

Chorus:
When it's springtime in the Rockies,
I am coming back to you,
Little sweetheart of the mountains,
With your bonny eyes of blue,
Once again, I'll say, "I love you,"
While the birds sing all the day,
When it's springtime in the Rockies,
In the Rockies, far away.

I've kept your image guarded in my heart, dear,
I've kept my love for you as pure as dew,
I'm longing for the time when I shall come, dear,
Back to that dear old western home and you,
I fancy it is springtime in the mountains,

The maple leaves in first sky—green appear,
I hear you softly say, my queen of May-time,
"This springtime you have come to meet me here."

Red River Valley

By Ethel Weehunt

*R*ed River Valley is a cowboy's love song, which originated in Canada with the Red River of the north. The song was honored when it also became a story of the Red River between Oklahoma and Texas, and gained wide appeal as one of the songs of cowboy life in cattle country.

The recordings of *Red River Valley*—first in 1925 by Texan Carl T. Sprague, and then by another Texan, Jules Verne Allen, four years later—boosted the song's popularity and established *Red River Valley* as an American cowboy song.

The lyrics are plaintive, as the cowboy accepts bravely the loneliness and pain of separation from his "darling." The song is easily sung; as you sing along with the melody, you feel the pangs of a heartbroken man, but somehow you do not doubt that he will again ride the green pastures as a rollicking cowboy. ❖

Red River Valley

From this valley they say you are going,
We will miss your bright eyes and sweet smile,
For they say you are taking the sunshine,
That has brightened our path for a while.

Chorus:
Come and sit by my side if you love me,
Do not hasten to bid me adieu,
Just remember the Red River Valley
And the cowboy that has loved you so true.

From this valley they say your are going,
I will miss your sweet face and your smile;
Just because you are weary and tired,
You are changing your range for a while.

O there never could be such a longing.
In the heart of a poor cowboy's breast,
That now dwells in the heart you are breaking,
As I wait in my home in the West.

Do you think of the valley you're leaving?
O how lonely and drear it will be!
Do you think of the kind heart your breaking?
And the pain you are causing to me?

As you go to your home by the ocean,
May you never forget those sweet hours,
That we spent in the Red River Valley,
And the love we exchanged mid the flowers.

The Magic Of Singing

By Edna Krause

We were a singing family and it was all because of Mama. At an early age, I noticed her face light up with a happy glow as she filled the kitchen on our Upper Michigan farm with joyous tunes.

How I wished I knew Mama's secret of the magic of singing! But she made no effort to encourage her large family to sing. Her joyful songs spoke louder than any lessons in music.

Is it any wonder that we all learned the fun of singing? It didn't matter how well we sang, nor even if we were on key. What mattered to us was how happy we felt as we sang.

We all sang for relaxation or to hear happy sounds. As much as we sang, none of us won any singing awards at school, church or anywhere else.

My older sister, Ginger, always sang the same songs, even when I visited her years after we both left home. And another sister, who shall remain nameless, liked to sing *Red Sails in the Sunset*. When she belted out the high notes, it sounded like car tires squealing around a corner at high speed. But it didn't matter. No one criticized her because she had the magic of singing.

The two who sang most often, alone or harmonizing together, were my sister Charlotte and I. When we were at the lower elementary age around 1940, we knew only bits and pieces of songs. Even so, we led the singing when my sisters and little brother, John, built a church out of hay bales. We all sat in our church on the bales and sang our hearts out because it was so near Easter Sunday.

How we liked to lie in the hayloft on a rainy day and sing! Sometimes there were five or six of us; other times, it was only Charlotte and me.

One day, Charlotte came home waving a sheet of paper and wearing a big grin. She had all the words to a song and she knew the tune! (I must add here that Charlotte learned a tune very easily and played the accordion by ear. I, on the other hand, found it difficult to learn a new song.)

The name of the new song was *Home on the Range*. I fell in love with the tune and the words immediately. They were so applicable to my way of life. I could relate to every sentence. The word "home" always fills me with warmth, security and

Quartet by Alan Foster © 1923 SEPS: Licensed by Curtis Publishing

thoughts of loving people. And in my mind, the "range" where "buffalo roam" was our farm where cattle and horses grazed. After years of watching our own cattle on government land, how could I not visualize calves and young heifers frolicking around while we harmonized with "Where the deer and the antelope play"?

I was beginning to think I was feeling the magic of singing, just like Mama did.

So we sang *Home on the Range* over and over. It was my favorite song, and it was Charlotte's favorite, too. The tune made harmonizing very easy and we enjoyed hearing ourselves sing. We sang for our own enjoyment in the attic, in the hay barn or in the apple orchard. We needed no audience.

It was understood in our family that no one sang for attention or to receive a compliment. No one needed to sing in the attic so the rest of the family couldn't hear. We all sang for relaxation or to hear happy sounds. As much as we sang, none of us won any singing awards at school, church or anywhere else.

We sang for fun, period. Oh, sometimes after a bad day in school or a sharp word at home, we sang to cheer ourselves up. It was then that I closed my eyes and drank in the comforting words:

"Where seldom is heard a discouraging word, And the skies are not cloudy all day."

Over and over we sang the refrain.

Charlotte sensed my need for the encouraging words that day and sang as long as I

wanted. And I did the same for her whenever she was down.

When I graduated from high school and left home, Charlotte was still a junior. I came home for Thanksgiving after being away for almost four months. I was anxious for a good songfest, and I saw that Charlotte felt the same way. So after visiting with the family a bit, Charlotte and I slipped away over the snow-covered yard into the warmth of the hayloft. There we snuggled into the soft hay and sang. The words to *Home on the Range* filled me with joy and contentment.

The name of the new song was **Home on the Range**. *I fell in love with the tune and the words immediately. They were so applicable to my way of life. I could relate to every sentence.*

We harmonized through all our favorites for old times' sake. But we started and ended our songfest with *Home on the Range*.

Later, when we were miles apart and seldom saw each other, we harmonized over the telephone.

We often spoke about the great gift Mama had passed on to us. And I was sure that now I knew Mama's secret of the magic of singing. ❖

Editor's note: Home on the Range *was originally a poem, written—as nearly as anyone can tell—in 1873 in Smith County, Kan. The words on the facing page are the original words to the poem, with the exception of the substitution of the popularly sung first line of the chorus, "Home, home on the range." In Dr. Higley's original poem, and as it was first performed after Dan Kelley added music a while later, the line went: "A home, a home/ Where the deer and the antelope play … ."*

The Western Home
(Home on the Range)

Words by Dr. Brewster Higley
Music by Daniel E. Kelley

Oh, give me a home
Where the buffalo roam,
Where the deer and the antelope play,
Where seldom is heard
A discouraging word,
And the sky is not cloudy all day.

Chorus:
Home, home on the range,
Where the deer and the antelope play,
Where never is heard a discouraging word,
And the sky is not cloudy all day.

Oh, give me the land
Where the bright diamond sand
Throws its light on the glittering stream
Where glideth along
The graceful white swan
Like a maid in her heavenly dream.

Oh, give me the gale
Of the Solomon vale
Where the life stream of buoyancy flows
On the banks of the Beaver
Where seldom, if ever
Any poisonous herbage doth grow.

I love the wild flowers
In this bright land of ours,
I love, too, the wild curlew's scream
The bluffs and white rocks
And antelope flocks,
That graze on the mountain so green.

How often at night
When the heavens were bright
By the light of the twinkling stars,
Have I stood here amazed
And asked as I gazed
If their glory exceeds that of ours.

The air is so clear,
The breeze so pure,
The zephyr so balmy and light;
I would not exchange
My home here on the range
Forever in azure so bright.

SONNY BOY

By Al Jolson, B.G. De Sylva, Lew Brown and Ray Henderson

Sonny Boy © 1928 by De Sylva, Brown & Henderson Inc., New York

Chorus:
When there are gray skies,
I don't mind the gray skies
You make them blue, Sonny Boy
Friends may forsake me
Let them all forsake me
You'll pull me through, Sonny Boy.
You're sent from Heaven
And I know your worth;
You've made a heaven
For me right here on earth!
When I'm old and gray, dear,
Promise you won't stray, dear,
I love you so, Sonny Boy.

You're my dearest prize, Sonny Boy;
Sent from out the skies, Sonny Boy
Let me hold you nearer
One thing makes you dearer:
You've your mother's eyes,
        Sonny Boy.

Second Chorus:
When there are gray skies,
I don't mind the gray skies
You make them blue, Sonny Boy
Friends may forsake me
Let them all forsake me
You'll pull me through, Sonny Boy.
You're sent from Heaven
And I know your worth;
You've made a heaven
For me right here on earth!
And then the angels grew lonely
Took you 'cause they're lonely
Now I'm lonely too, Sonny Boy.

Climb upon my knee, Sonny Boy;
You are only three, Sonny Boy
You've no way of knowing
There's no way of showing
What you mean to me, Sonny Boy.

Shenandoah

Editor's note: There are two ideas as to how e came to have this very popular folk song. ne has it that the song was originally the story f a white trader and his love for the daughter f an Indian chieftain, Shenandoah (for whom a ver was named). "The wide Missouri" refers the Missouri River. The other holds that the ong was originated by homesick settlers mov-g westward who remembered their loved ones ack in the Shenandoah Valley.

Oh, Shenandoah, I long to hear you,
Away! You rolling river,
Oh, Shenandoah, I long to hear you,
Away, we're bound away,
'Cross the wide Missouri.

Oh Shenandoah, I love your daughter,
Away, you rolling river,
Just for her, I crossed the water,
Away, we're bound away,
'Cross the wide Missouri.

Farewell, my love, I'm bound to leave you,
Away, you rolling river,
Shenandoah, I'll not deceive you,
Away, we're bound away,
'Cross the wide Missouri.

Down in the Valley

Editor's note: Like so many ld-time songs, there are many ersions of Down in the Valley. ne popular theory is that the ong was written by a prisoner the Raleigh State Prison as a letter to a girl in Alabama.

Chorus:
Down in the valley,
The valley so low,
Hang your head over,
Hear the winds blow.
Hear the winds blow, dear,
Hear the winds blow.
Hang your head over,
Hear the winds blow.

Give my heart ease, love,
Oh give my heart ease.
Think of me darling,
Oh give my heart ease.
Write me a letter,
And send it by mail
Send it in care of
Birmingham Jail.

Write me a letter,
With just a few lines,
Answer me, darling,
Will you be mine?
Roses love sunshine,
Violets love dew,
Angels in heaven
Know I love you!

This gloomy prison,
Is far from you, dear,
But not forever,
I'm out in a year,
I make this promise
To go straight and true,
And for a lifetime
To love only you.

If you don't love me,
Love whom you please,
Throw your arms round me,
Give my heart ease.
Give my heart ease, dear,
Give my heart ease,
Throw your arms round me,
Give my heart ease.

Throw your arms round me,
Before it's too late;
Throw your arms round me,
Feel my heart break.
Feel my heart break, dear,
Feel my heart break.
Throw your arms round me,
Feel my heart break.

Rock Me to Sleep

By Olive Workman Persinger as told to Donna McGuire Tann...

I grew up in the 1930s in the area of Kaymoore, W.Va. Papa was a minister and Mama was a traditional preacher's wife. She loved to sing in church, and she passed this love down to her children, including me.

As I grew into a teen, I was a faithful listener of both th... *Old Farm Hour* on WCHS in Charleston, W.Va., and the *Jam... boree* on WWVA in Wheeling, W.Va. I could only dream of being as talented as those I listened to on the radio. I practiced for hours, singing the songs I had heard, and I learned to accompany myself with a guitar.

In 1938, when I was 16 years old, I heard that entertainers from WCHS and WWVA were coming to perform at a park in Summers... ville, W.Va. With guitar in hand and stars in my eyes, I was there waiting for them when that day arrived.

I was overwhelmed; now I was seeing an... hearing all my favorite radio performers in person. Then, when the call came out for any local people to sing, I was there. After I had finished, I was happy. My dream had come true; I had sung with the best.

> *I was overwhelmed; I saw and heard now all my favorite radio performers in person. My dream had come true; I had sung with the best.*

Then the well-known entertainer Lee Moore approached me. "Would you be interested in auditioning at WCHS?" he asked

I was almost speechless. Boy, would I ever!

I made the 50-mile trip from my home in Fayetteville to Charleston. I was a very nervous girl when I was left alone in a room with just a microphone. I had been instructed to simply start singing when I saw the red light come on.

I stared at that light. When it turned red, I sang an earnest, hear... felt rendition of *Rock Me to Sleep in My Rocky Mountain Home*. And when I finished, I was welcomed into the family of entertaine... on the WCHS *Old Farm Hour*. Eventually I moved on to WWVA'... *Wheeling Jamboree*.

I cherish my memories of my time with all those well-known personalities whose elite membership I was lucky enough to join. The song *Rock Me to Sleep in My Rocky Mountain Home* placed m... right in the middle of a wish fulfilled, doing something I still love t... do—*sing*. ❖

Rock Me to Sleep in My Rocky Mountain Home

Words by Robert E. Harty
Music by Harold Dixon

Ev'ry time I see the golden sunset
  in the west,
With each memory comes a melody,
I can hear my rocky mountains ever
  calling me,
Life is filled with sadness
But there's gladness waiting there
  for me.

Chorus:
Rock me to sleep in my rocky
  mountain home,
I want to lay my weary head
Upon my mammy's feather bed.
Just let me stray
Where the silv'ry moonbeams
  play …
I hear the night birds humming
And I'm coming tho' you're
  far away …
Sis and brother, dad and
  mother by the cabin door,
Golden sunbeams,
  happy daydreams,
Come to me once more …
So won't you
Rock me to sleep in my rocky
  mountain home?
Just let me live there,
  love there,
Never no more to roam.

Like a gypsy I've been roaming on
  a lonesome trail,
Over hill and vale, but I always fail,
For the rainbow has no ending;
  happiness is truth …

Rock Me to Sleep in my Rocky Mountain Home 1922 © Dixon-Lane Music Pub. Co., Chicago

Now my heart is yearning
And I'm turning back to days of youth.

A Special Day,
A Special Song

By Dorothy Camp Berryma

*I*n 1939, I was 18 years old and got my first steady job in downtown Chicago. It felt so good to be able to bring home a paycheck and hand it to my widowed mother. She had sacrificed so much to see that my two younger sisters and would be educated enough to make our way in the world.

I was a secretary in an office building, and during my lunch hour, I often strolled along State Street to read the playbills in front of the Chicago Theater. I always hoped that I could put aside enough money from my allowance to treat Mom to a matinee there and dinner later.

The Chicago usually showed a first-class movie and occasionally invited a special guest star to stage a live act. Once they featured a popular new singer, Frank Sinatra, and I almost passed out at the thought of seeing him onstage. But my plan remained out of reach for nearly a year after finding work.

At last the time came when I had saved up $15. Around that same time, I saw that in addition to the movie that week, *Goodbye, Mr. Chips*, the live guest performer at the Chicago would be Bob Hope.

Mom and I had heard Bob on the radio and we loved his humor. We were very excited at the prospect of our special treat! On a Saturday afternoon that summer, we made the trolley trip downtown to see the matinee. Afterward we planned to walk across the street to Reick's Beanery where the food was excellent and the prices right. Mom assured me that if we spent more than my limit she had saved a few dollars just in case.

Even now, so many years later, whenever I play that song on my small electronic organ, I think of our special day and how proud I was to be able to give back a little something to Mother for all she had done.

It was such a pleasure for me not only to see Mom enjoy her favorite kind of movie—a tearjerker—but also to see her dark eyes sparkle and her face light up with laughter at Bob Hope's songs, snappy patter and soft-shoe dancing.

Then he held up his hands and the audience settled down so he coul introduce his lovely wife, Dolores. He stood proudly by while she sang a beautiful song, *Imagination*, in her lovely voice. The applause was thunderous.

Later, Mom said, "Thanks, Dorothy, for this special day. But do you want to know what I enjoyed most?"

"Bob Hope?" I asked.

"Well, yes, I did enjoy him a lot," she said. "But I never knew that his wife had such a beautiful singing voice. When she sang that song, *Imagination*, it was simply thrilling. I'll never forget it."

Afterward, although I could not find a recording of the song sung by Dolores Hope, I did find a recording by an orchestra. We often played it on our Victrola, and whenever we heard it, Mom got that same dreamy look on her face. Then I knew she was reliving our special day.

My sisters and I memorized the words to *Imagination,* and I learned to play it on our old upright piano. When we sisters invited friends for a songfest, Mom would say, "Kids, you know what I want to hear." And we would gladly oblige by singing *Imagination*.

Even now, so many years later, whenever I play that song on my small electronic organ, I think of our special day and how proud I was to be able to give back a little something to Mother for all she had done.

Bob Hope celebrated his 100th birthday in 2003 with his devoted wife, Dolores, still at his side. Within three months, we had lost him. Whenever I hear tributes to Bob, in my mind I also hear Dolores Hope's beautiful rendition of *Imagination*, and I pay tribute to the joy she, too, gave Mother and me in those Good Old Days. ❖

Imagination

Imagination is funny …
It makes a cloudy day sunny …
Makes a bee think of honey …
Just as I think of you.

Imagination—it's so crazy …
Your whole perspective gets hazy …
Starts you asking a daisy what to do,
    what to do.
Have you ever felt the gentle touch and
    then a kiss and then and then
Find it's only your imagination again?
    Oh well …

Imagination is silly …
You go around willy-nilly …
For example, I go around wanting you
And yet I can't imagine that you—
Can't imagine that you—
Can't imagine that you want me, too.

The great entertainer and comedian Bob Hope sits at a table with his wife, singer Dolores Hope, at a formal dinner function, circa 1948.
Hulton Archive/Getty Images.

Songs of Love

Chapter Two

Janice was 17 when I asked her to marry me, and I was the ripe old age of 20. If my own children had been that age approaching the holy state of matrimony, I would have fainted or grabbed my shotgun, whichever would have occurred to me first. Back in the Good Old Days, however, it wasn't particularly uncommon to marry, as we did a year later, at the ages of 18 and 21.

Our early years together were not easy. More times than I care to remember our dollars were measured in single digits. Those were the days of beans and cornbread suppers (cornbread and milk lunches also, I might add). That rarely discouraged us. We were young. We were optimistic. We were in love. Surely with that we would overcome all obstacles.

Surprisingly, we did overcome most, partly with the help of a song. The first time I heard it was on the radio. It was a song of love, framed with the hope and idealism of youth. I learned later that the song's words and music were by Harry Woods. It was called *Side By Side*:

Side By Side
See that sun in the morning
Peeking over the hill
I'll bet you're sure it always has
And sure it always will
That's how I feel about someone,
How somebody feels about me
We're sure we love each other
That's the way we'll always be:

We're all hunting for something
Something we don't know what
'Cause none of us are satisfied
With things we know we've got.
We all forgot about moonlight
As soon as we've given our vow
But we'd all be so happy
If we'd start and sing right now:

Chorus:
Oh! we ain't got a barrel of money,
Maybe we're ragged and funny,
But we'll travel along, singin' a song
Side by side.
Don't know what's comin' tomorrow,
Maybe it's trouble and sorrow,
But we'll travel the road, sharin' our load
Side by side.
Through all kinds of weather
What if the sky should fall
Just as long as we're together,
It doesn't matter at all
When they've all had their quarrels
and parted
We'll be the same as we started
Just trav'lin' along, singin' a song
Side by side.

I can't say that *Side By Side* became "our song," but at least it became the song we lived by. We saw tough times wreak havoc on marriages all around us. So, early on, we decided we would live our life together by the words of that popular song.

I brought Janice flowers—wildflowers from alongside the road or roses from her own flower bed. We enjoyed picnics when we couldn't afford restaurants. We tried to meet every day head on, knowing we could count on one another being there.

Nowadays things are a lot better. I buy flowers from florists who didn't even exist when Janice and I first wed. We can afford to go out to restaurants, but I still like picnics with the love of my life. Even though we awaken with a few more aches and pains, we still try to meet every morning with joy and optimism.

So, I guess we'll keep travelin' our road, sharin' our load, and the song I'll be humming will be *Side By Side*, one of our Songs of Love from the Good Old Days.

—*Ken Tate, Edito*

Side By Side

Words & Music by
Harry Woods

HORACE WRIGHT & RENE DIETRICH
THE SOMEWHAT DIFFERENT SINGERS

Shapiro, Bernstein & Co.
MUSIC PUBLISHERS
Cor. Broadway & 47th Street
New York
Reg. U.S. Pat. Off.

Our Love Song Was *My Happiness*

By Audrey Carli

The love song *My Happiness* was popular in early 1949 when Dave and I met at a school dance in Wakefield, our northern Michigan town. The soft, romantic lyrics were wafting from the jukebox. The sweet words melted in me as I realized Dave was special, someone I would like to date regularly if he felt the same way. Oh well, in time we would know what the future held for us.

After that, whenever *My Happiness* sounded on my family's radio, I thought about Dave's blue eyes, deep voice and endearing smile. When I was ready to study and was about to turn off the radio, I listened a while longer if that long song flowed forth.

Soon Dave and I rode to picnics, concerts, to my grandparents' and other relatives' homes for picnics or dinners. And we exchanged smiles and listened intently to *My Happiness* whenever the popular melody filled the car.

Then, finally, when we knew we might want to marry someday, Dave had to leave our Michigan town to attend Marquette University in Milwaukee. I was going to Duluth, Minn., with my friends, Marilyn and Dorothy, to work in an office.

When it was time for Dave and me to say good-bye—possibly for forever as our lives went their separate ways—we danced again to *My Happiness*. And the lyrics "Evening shadows make me blue when each weary day is through, how I long to be with you, my happiness" sank into my heart and wept there with the loneliness I would feel—and the loneliness Dave whispered, warming my ear, that he would feel.

At that time, however, neither of us had jobs or savings to support marriage. So we stood under the porch light at my white frame home and told each other we hoped to someday resume our dating.

We had memorized the last words of *My Happiness*, and that night they were also our romantic dream: "Whether skies are gray or blue, any place on earth will do, just as long as I'm with you, my happiness."

But soon we were miles apart, pursuing that particular chapter in each or our lives. We wrote letters because in 1950, long-distance phone calls were costly. I also wrote to friends in my hometown.

My happiness soared when I received an invitation to my friend Alice's August wedding! Being a romantic, I wrote to Alice that I'd be there, but I'd not have a guest. Dave was too far away to attend, I was sure. It cost too much money to take the train to a wedding on a college student's restricted funds.

As the summer melted away, Marilyn, Dorothy and I went to Park Point for picnics on Sunday afternoons. We browsed at the Glass Block department store. We managed to go out for an occasional hamburger, too. And sometimes *My Happiness* poured out of a radio or store speaker—and loneliness gnawed at me.

The night before Alice's wedding, I boarded the bus at Duluth, Minn., and rode home to Wakefield.

At the wedding, I gazed at Alice and Jim as they stood at the altar and exchanged their wedding vows. I thought about "Someday, maybe …" for Dave and me. Then dread filled me. *What if he had met someone else? What if he had lost interest? Was I living on a romantic dream that was dying daily?*

I was so engrossed in my thoughts that I didn't notice that someone had slipped into the pew beside me until he poked my arm. Then I stared straight into Dave's shimmering blue eyes and vibrant smile.

Later he told me, "Alice sent me an invitation and hoped I'd be able to come and surprise you. I've been working at temporary jobs whenever possible. So I had train fare."

At the wedding reception that night, I was again dancing with Dave—and when *My Happiness* filled the hall, we exchanged gazes. In that moment, I knew that Dave and I would someday dance at our own wedding.

And we did. ❖

My Happiness

*By Betty Peterson Music
and Borney Bergantine*

Evening shadows
    make me blue,
When each weary day
    is through,
How I long to be with you,
My happiness!

Ev'ry day I reminisce,
Dreaming of your tender kiss,
Always thinking how I miss
My happiness.

A million years it seems
Have gone by since we
    shared our dreams,
But I'll hold you again,
There'll be no blue
    memories then.

Whether skies are gray
    or blue,
Any place on earth will do,
Just as long as I'm with you,
My happiness!

Out on a Date by John LaGatta © 1934 SEPS: Licensed by Curtis Publishing

Yankee Rose

By Al Size

This is about my 75-year love affair with Yankee Rose. I never met her in the flesh; she was just a girl in a popular song. But what a girl she was!

We older folks often find that songs from bygone years linger in our memories. Sometimes the tune is widely popular, like *Sweet Sue*. Other times it holds special appeal for just a few individuals. For me, there is one tune whose words and music are still fresh in my mind, although I'm willing to admit that they faded from my contemporaries' recollections long ago.

Yankee Rose came out in 1926, when I was 10 years old. Composed by Abe Frankl with words by Sidney Holden, it was published by Irving Berlin's music company. It enjoyed brief popularity and then disappeared from public attention—but not from mine.

> *I was patriotic. I loved the picture of Yankee Rose on the sheet music; I saw it in the 5-and-10-cent store and quickly memorized the words.*

I was patriotic. I loved the picture of Yankee Rose on the sheet music; I saw it in the 5-and-10-cent store and quickly memorized the words. They have remained with me for a lifetime.

I had a special reason for being smitten with *Yankee Rose*. It reminded me of Dorothy, a girl on whom I had my first real crush in junior high school. Dorothy also had the clear, innocent features and bobbed hair of Yankee Rose, as did many young women in the 1920s.

For an all-too-brief period, I was able to hear my favorite song on my dad's radio, played by Sam Lanin's orchestra, better known as the Ipana Troubadours. May Singhi Breen, an early radio star, also performed a ukulele arrangement of the tune. But through the years, the only rendition of the song I heard was my own, usually in the shower.

I couldn't get it out of my mind. In my retirement years I finally obtained a tape of the Revelers, a long-gone singing group, performing *Yankee Rose*. To tell the truth, I prefer my own rendition—although my long-persecuted wife, who has a background as a singer, does not.

People who heard of my obsession tried to help me by contributing information. One former professional dancer told me that "*Yankee Rose* was great for tap dancing, too."

I guess this octogenarian's love affair with Yankee Rose will continue to the end. When I compare her looks to some of the gals I see in today's movies and on television, I don't think there's any chance of my being unfaithful. ❖

YANKEE ROSE

Words by Sidney Holden,
Music by Abe Frankl

We've seen roses grow
Almost ev'rywhere,
But you're one we place apart,
For there's none we've found
Who is half so fair,
As our own sweet heart:

Yankee Rose so true,
How we all love you,
And we're proud to say
You belong to the U.S.A.
Yankee Rose we call
Sweetest rose of all,
And thru' strife and care,
You're always there,
That's why we'll always love you
Yankee Rose

Where the Hudson flows,
There's a diff'rent rose,
And they call her "Liberty,"
Let me say to you
She's Red, White and Blue,
You'll agree with me:

Yankee Rose so true,
She's a beaut' in that pose,
Here's my hand, my heart,
I'll play my part,
And so will ev'ry
Yankee Rose.

Yankee Rose © 1926 by Irving Berlin Inc., New York

Remembering Nelson Eddy

By Mary B. Bem

When I'm calling you-ooo-ooo, Will you answer too-ooo-ooo? If you grew up during the 1930s and '40s, no doubt you recall Nelson Eddy singing those words from *Indian Love Call* to Jeanette MacDonald in the movie musical *Rose Marie*. That velvety baritone made him famous before films, and his dashing good looks and charming personality won him fans everywhere, me among them.

I was so taken with him that I saw all of his movies and bought all his records. As a cub reporter in Canton, Ohio, when I learned that he was going

A publicity photograph of Nelson Eddy and Jeanette MacDonald.

to appear there in concert, I made sure I was going. And amazingly, when the editor heard of my interest, he asked me to interview Nelson.

I could hardly believe my good luck! But sure enough, on the day of his performance, March 24, 1952, Nelson granted me an interview and even posed for a picture with his accompanist.

Those blue eyes were even more brilliant in person. He was so pleasant and entertaining in his conversation that it was easy to realize that the charm he displayed on the big screen was genuine. I was nervous about talking to someone of his stature, but he pretended not to notice and made me feel truly at ease. He told me that he had only one word of advice for ambitious young musicians: "Work."

I was surprised to learn that he had had to drop out of school and work hard to achieve his place in film history. But his efforts paid off: He was the highest-paid singer in the world for 14 years!

"There's no such thing as luck or short-cuts," he said. "It takes plenty of hard work, time and experience. It doesn't make any difference who the person is or where he lives—if he has talent and works hard, he's bound to get somewhere." Those words have always been an inspiration to me.

As proof of his large following, some 1,000 members of his fan club from all over the country had come to his recital in Canton. He was very kind and gracious to them, talking to them personally afterward and giving them a special pen that he used to autograph their programs.

Nelson had just started a concert tour. He was one of the first Hollywood musical stars to take this step. He loved singing, and it was evident in his performance that night.

Someday, he told me, he would probably retire and hang out a shingle reading "Singing Lessons Given Here." But he never had to worry about retiring. He found success in nightclubs and theaters; in fact, he died while performing onstage one night in Miami in 1967.

In my work over the years, I met other celebrities. But I remember Nelson Eddy as the kindest and most gracious of them all. He was a true professional, but also a most humble being. ❖

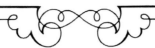

Indian Love Call

Words by Otto Harbach and Oscar Hammerstein
Music by Rudolf Friml

When I'm calling you-oo-oo-oo …
Will you answer too-oo-oo-oo?
That means I offer
My love to you
To be your own.
If you refuse me
I will be blue
And waiting all alone.

But if when you hear
My love call ringing clear
And I hear
Your answering echo, so dear,
Then I will know
Our love will come true,
You'll belong to me,
I'll belong to you.

Nelson Eddy croons to Jeanette MacDonald in a publicity poster from one of their films.

Let Me Call You Sweetheart

By Winnie Rhoades Schuetz

In the summer of 1951, a southern Illinois farmhand arrived as a hitchhiker in Rockford, Ill. His worldly goods consisted of a cheap dress suit, a cardboard suitcase containing his work clothes and 3 cents cash in his pocket. By nightfall he had a job and a place to stay.

Lewis Schuetz was 22 years old and had worked full time, mostly on the farm, since he graduated from eighth grade at age 14. He had a talent with mechanical things and knew how to milk cows. His new job was working for a custom harvester, running a corn sheller. Besides paying him wages, the job provided him with a room, meals and laundry, as was the custom in those days.

Lewis and the boss hit it off. At that time, the boss was coaching a 4-H girls' softball team. In time, Lewis began to help coach the team. One evening at suppertime, the boss mentioned that the 4-H fair was starting that night, and he asked Lewis if he wanted to go along.

While Lewis was helping coach the team, he had spotted a girl he wanted to meet. But somehow, that wish had not materialized. Then, while he was walking around the fairgrounds, Lewis saw Janice, one of the girls he knew from his team, and, wonder of wonders, she was talking to "the girl." Lewis walked right up and spoke to Janice, and naturally, he was introduced to her companion. That is when I met Lewis, and once I looked into those blue, blue eyes, I was a gonner!

He ended up walking Janice and me home, and so learned where I lived. About a week later, as I was walking to our mailbox across the road from my house, a big farm truck screeched to a stop close to me. Looking up, I recognized Lewis in the driver's seat. He told me he was taking a load of apples to the cider press outside town. Then he asked me out on a date to go to the movies.

On Sunday afternoon, we walked down to the bus stop. The weather was warm and balmy. But by the time we came out of the theater, it was raining cats and dogs. We both got soaking wet walking back to my house from the bus stop.

The next time Lewis and I went on a date, he pulled up in the driveway in a 1939 Chevy. Then we went out in style.

For some time, a group of my friends had been going to a barn dance every Saturday night at Theodorf's barn out at Pecatonica, Ill. That was a special place. No liquor was sold. The ticket taker was the bouncer and he was a big man. He also happened to be a very good friend of mine and looked out for us young kids. My dad usually took us out there and made arrangements with somebody to bring us home because we were all too young to drive.

The first time Lewis took the gang out to the dance, they played *Let Me Call You Sweetheart* for our first dance. That became our song.

After awhile, Lewis and I went shopping for an engagement ring. We picked out a nice one in a low price range. I was looking forward to seeing it on Christmas, but I got another gift instead. I got another gift.

Finally, the time came when Lewis wanted to give me the ring, but it wasn't paid off. So he borrowed enough from his future father-in-law to get it. On April 6, 1952, he asked me that all-important question. That Saturday night, we announced our engagement, and the band played our song as we waltzed across the dance floor while all our friends cheered us.

We were married at my home church, Messiah Lutheran Church, in the west end of Rockford. It was a simple ceremony with Janice as my maid of honor and Lewis' co-worker (and my next-door neighbor) Bob as the best man. We honeymooned in Wisconsin. But first we danced to our song at Theordorf's barn dance. Our wedding day was June 21, 1952, which also was the longest day of the year.

Lewis had been paying on a small, 18-foot trailer, and we moved right in when we got back from our honeymoon. The trailer was parked on a rented lot, but during an unexpected flood, we were forced to move onto a lot my dad owned.

We hardly ever missed a Saturday night at Theodorf's until the babies began coming. By then Lewis was working as a dairy herdsman. Still, whenever we could get a babysitter, we always went back to our favorite dance hall. When we were married 10 years, Lewis bought me a beautiful music box that played *Let Me Call You Sweetheart*. I still treasure it.

When we celebrated our 25th anniversary, we had a supper and dance. By that time we were living in southern Illinois not too far from his hometown of Venedy, and Lewis was working at a printing company at Sparta. For our first dance they played our song, and we whirled away in each other's arms, surrounded by our five children and several grandchildren, secure in God's blessings.

We were married a month short of 49 years, best friends, lovers, parents, and friends to many, secure in our love for each other, when Lewis went home to be with our Lord.

I stayed with him in the hospital the last two nights. I stood by his bed, holding his hand. He seemed improved. He told me some things he had on his mind—about what he wanted me to do when he was gone. I just didn't realize how quickly he would be gone.

I tried to lay down on my makeshift bed, but he was so restless that I got up again. He began singing Hank Williams' *Lovesick Blues* to me.

Then he sang our song, and he told me how much he loved me and what a good wife and mother I was.

"Mom, I wish you could go with me," he said suddenly, "but I don't want you to die to do it." I just couldn't accept what was happening.

Soon his doctor came in and checked him. "Winnie," she said, "you need to call your family." Then she took me in her arms and we stood there silently. The long battle was done. My sweetheart went to heaven on May 23, 2001.

These days I often find myself singing our song as I go about my daily routine, and I can strongly feel him by my side. When I play my music box, I remember all our wonderful years, loving and living, good times and bad. I can't believe it went so fast. Then I think back to that 25th anniversary evening when we danced to our song and Lewis held me in his arms as he whispered in my ear, "You'll always be my sweetheart." Right up to the last, he always made me feel just like I was. ❖

Let Me Call You Sweetheart

Words by Beth Slater Whitson
Music by Leo Friedman (1910)

I am dreaming, Dear, of you
Day by day,
Dreaming when the skies are blue,
When they're gray;
When the silv'ry moonlight gleams,
Still I wander on in dreams
In a land of love, it seems,
Just with you

Chorus:
Let me call you "Sweetheart,"
I'm in love with you.
Let me hear you whisper that you love me too.

Keep the love-light glowing in your eyes so true
Let me call you "Sweetheart,"
I'm in love with you!

Longing for you all the while,
More and more;
Longing for the sunny smile I adore;
Birds are singing far and near,
Roses blooming ev'rywhere
You, alone, my heart can cheer;
You, just you.

Repeat Chorus

Two Little Girls In Blue

An old man gazed on a photograph,
In a locket he'd worn for years,
His nephew then asked him the
   reason why
This picture had caused him tears.
"Just listen," he said, "and I'll tell
   you, lad,
A story that's strange, but true,
Your father and I, at the school,
   one day—
Met two little girls in blue.

Chorus:
Two little girls in blue, lad,
Two little girls in blue,
They were sisters, we were brothers,
And learned to love those two.
One little girl in blue, lad,
Who won your father's heart,
Became your mother,
I married the other—
But we have drifted apart.

That picture was one of those
   girls," he said,
"And to me she was once
   a wife,
I thought her unfaithful, we
   quarreled, lad—
And parted that night for life.
My fancy or jealousy wronged
   a heart,
A heart that was good and true,
For two better girls never lived, than they—
Those two little girls in blue."

Repeat Chorus

THE EDWARD B. MARKS SERIES OF
UNFORGETTABLE SONGS OF AMERICA

Two Little Girls In Blue

Words and Music by
CHAS. GRAHAM
GEO. L. SPALDING
W. B. GRAY

PRICE 50¢

WHEN PERFORMING THIS COMPOSITION KINDLY GIVE ALL PROGRAM CREDITS TO

EDWARD B. MARKS MUSIC CORPORATION
RCA BUILDING · RADIO CITY · NEW YORK
For a list of additional unforgettable
Old Time Songs see back page

Two Little Girls in Blue © 1893 by Spaulding & Kornder

1938 *Farmer's Wife*, House of White Birches nostalgia archives

Remembering Lilli Marlene

By Vincent Argondezzi

It was the single most popular song of World War II. The name was spelled and pronounced in slightly different ways—"Lili Marlene," "Lily Marlene" and "Lily Marlene," among others—but the words captured the heart of the world and expressed the yearning and hope that peace would be found at the garden gate where all the Lilli Marlenes waited with loving hearts.

I heard it sung by Marlene Dietrich. It captured my heart, but only after meeting several German soldiers did I really feel the power and beauty of *Lilli Marlene.*

After the war, one of the duties I shared with a few other American soldiers was escorting German soldiers, who were waiting to be repatriated, to a work area.

The Germans never wasted a chance to sing about Lilli Marlene, and they did so with such compelling emotion that it created the illusion that music and love now had replaced anger and hate in the conscience of a world at peace.

Many years have gone by since *Lilli Marlene* captured the hearts of the world, but I still find myself humming it and singing it, just as I did those many years ago, my "Lilli of the lamplight." ❖

Lilli Marlene

English lyrics by Tommie Connor (1944)
Original German lyrics by Hans Leip
Music by Norbert Schultze (1938)

Underneath the lantern,
By the barrack gate,
Darling, I remember
The way you used to wait,
'Twas there that you whispered tenderly
That you loved me,
You'd always be
My Lilli of the lamplight,
My own Lilli Marlene.

Time would come for roll call,
Time for us to part,
Darling, I'd caress you,
And press you to my heart,
And there, 'neath the far-off lantern light,
I'd hold you tight,
We'd kiss all night,
My Lilli of the lamplight,
My own Lilli Marlene.

Orders came for sailing,
Somewhere over there,
All confined to barracks
Was more than I could bear.
I knew you were waiting in the street,
I heard your feet,
But could not meet
My Lilli of the lamplight,
My own Lilli Marlene.

Resting in a billet,
Just behind the line,
Even tho' we're parted,
Your lips are close to mine.
You wait where the lantern softly gleams,
Your sweet face seems
To haunt my dreams,
My Lilli of the lamplight,
My own Lilli Marlene.

You Made Me Love You

Words by Joseph McCarthy
Music by James V. Monaco

You made me love you,
I didn't wanna do it,
I didn't wanna do it,
You made me want you
And all the time you knew it,
I guess you always knew it.

You made me happy, sometimes,
You made me glad,
But there were times, dear,
You made me feel so bad.

You made me sigh for
I didn't wanna tell you,
I didn't wanna tell you,

I want some love that's true,
Yes, I do, 'deed I do, you know I do.
Gimme, gimme, gimme, gimme what
    I cry for,
You know you got the brand
Of kisses that I'd die for …
You know you made me love you.

You made me love you
I didn't wanna do it,
I didn't wanna do it,
You made me want you
And all the time you knew it,
I guess you always knew it.

The Girl I Left Behind Me

The dames of France are fond and free,
And Flemish lips are willing,
And soft the maids of Italy,
And Spanish eyes are thrilling;
Still though I bask beneath their smile,
Their charms fail to bind me,
And my heart falls back to Erin's Isle,
To the girl I left behind me.

For she's fair as Shannon's side,
And purer than its water,
But she refused to be my bride
Though many a year I sought her;
Yet, since to France I sail'd away,
Her letters oft' remind me,
That I promised never to gainsay
The girl I left behind me.

She says, "My own dear love, come home,
My friends are rich and many,
Or else abroad with you I'll roam,
A soldier stout as any;
If you'll not come, nor let me go,
I'll think you have resigned me."
My heart nigh broke when I answered "No"
To the girl I left behind me.

For never shall my true love brave
A life of war and toiling,
And never as a skulking slave
I'll tread my native soil on;
But were it free or to be freed,
The battle's close would find me
To Ireland bound, nor message need
From the girl I left behind me.

Peg O' My Heart

By Janice Julius

My mother's name was Margaret Hogan. She was born in Urbana, Ill., in 1909, a red-haired, blue-eyed, third child of second-generation Irish immigrants.

The name Margaret has several nicknames, such as Margie, Peggy and Peg. Different friends and family called my mom Peggy, but when she grew up, it was changed to a more adult Peg.

She had a strong bond with her Irish heritage and loved the lilting melodies of Irish songs. After my parents were married, Dad would sing *Peg O' My Heart* to her on her birthday and their anniversary.

Every year at our family reunion, we had sing-alongs. Many in our family played guitars and banjos, and they took requests. We sang every song anyone knew, and it wasn't a complete day without singing *Peg O' My Heart* at the top of our lungs.

One day in 1941, Mom and I were sitting on a blanket in the back yard when, all of a sudden, the strains of *Peg O' My Heart* came from inside the house. We didn't have a piano, so we hurried in to see where the music was coming from.

There was my dad, pumping away on a player piano that someone had given him! Who would have guessed that they also had the roll of music for *Peg O' My Heart*? Two of us kids took over the pumping while Dad and Mom danced around the living room as Dad sang *Peg O' My Heart* in her ear.

I came to love this song, too, because it reminded me, in a very special way, of how my dad told my mom that he loved her.

Forty-eight years later, I could almost feel her there when we played *Peg O' My Heart* at her memorial service. She was the Peg of our hearts, too. ❖

Peggy O'Neil © 1921 by Leo Feist, Inc., New York

Peg O' My Heart

Words by Alfred Bryan
Music by Fred Fisher

Peg o' my heart, I love you,
We'll never part, for I love you,
Dear little girl, sweet little girl,
Sweeter than the rose of Erin
It's the shamrock we'll be sharing.
Peg o' my heart, your glances
My Irish heart entrances.
Come be my own
Come make your home
In my heart.

I'm Knee Deep in Daisies

(And Head Over Heels in Love)

Words by Joe Goodwin, George A. Little and Jack Stanley
Music by Paul Ash and Larry Shay

I just got a funny letter
From a pal who went away,
He's on a short vacation
A little recreation
Guess my pal is feeling better
Here is what he's got to say,
"I won't come back,
No, I won't come back,
I'm down here to stay."

Chorus:
"I'm knee deep in daisies
And head over heels in love.
Oh, I'm acting like a clown,
In a little one horse town,
I'm hazy,
I'm crazy
I guess that I'm in love.
She's just a farmer's
daughter,
But say, old pay, you
oughter meet her,
Ev'ry evening in the
moonlight
Down by the old mill
stream.
While she's dreamin'
I am schemin'
You know what I mean,
I'm fallin',
I'm fallin',
And I don't need a shove,
Because I'm knee deep
in daisies
And head over heels
in love."

"Lots of fun around a farmyard,
While a fellow's raisin' things,
I even raise the dickens
While I am raisin' chickens,
And besides my little sweetheart,
Got a cow named Sally Green,
I'll tell you what,
When the weather's hot,
She gives good ice cream."

Repeat Chorus

Down by the Old Mill Stream

Words and music by John Read

You must know that my uncle is a farmer,
Keeps a large farm in the West;
While staying there I met a little charmer,
And many a time I caressed
That girl so fair, with nut-brown hair;
Her equal ne'er was seen,
And where I met this charming little pet,
Was down by the old mill stream—Ah!

Chorus:
Down by the old mill stream,
There many happy hours I've been seen,
Strolling day by day, we passed the time away,
Down by the old mill stream.

Her father was the owner of a dairy,
Her brother worked the plough,
And while I used to roam with little Mary,
Her mother would milk the cow;
But her father said we should not wed,
Which I thought rather mean;
As she could not be my wife, she said she'd
        end her life
By drowning in the old mill stream.

Now the old man laughed at his daughter,
Saying, "I don't believe a word you say,"
But when he saw her struggling in the water,
He exclaimed, "Do save her, pray!"
But it was too late; she had met her fate;
Oh, what terrible scene!
The old man cried as the neighbors tried
To pull her out of the stream.

At last they got her out of the water,
And some of the neighbors said,
"Oh, Brown, you've been the ruin of your
        daughter,
For the girl is really dead!"
He tore his hair, gave way to despair,
While my love I pulled from the stream;
And now we're wed, and it well is said,
Two happier ne'er was seen.

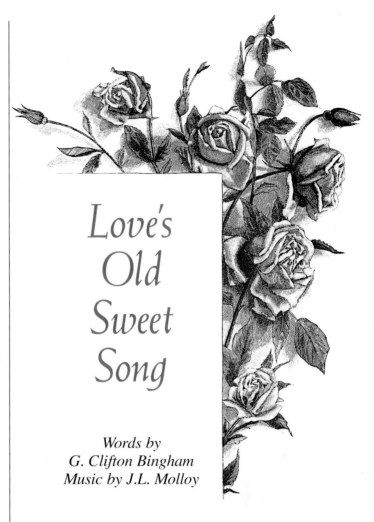

Love's Old Sweet Song

Words by
G. Clifton Bingham
Music by J.L. Molloy

Once in the dear dead days beyond recall,
When on the world the mists began to fall,
Out of the dreams that rose in happy throng,
Low, to our hearts love sang an old sweet song.
And in the dusk, where fell the firelight's gleam,
Softly it wove itself into our dream.

Chorus:
Just a song at twilight, when the lights are low,
And the flick'ring shadows softly come and go;
Tho' the heart be weary, sad the day and long,
Still to us at twilight comes love's old song,
Comes love's old sweet song.

Even today we hear love's song of yore,
Deep in our hearts it dwells forevermore,
Footsteps may falter, weary grows the way,
Still we can hear it at the close of day;
So till the end, when life's dim shadows fall,
Love will be found in the sweetest song of all.

Tying the Leaves

By Alan Mann

The popularity of a musical hit from early in the 20th century is still demonstrated by the number of queries for its lyrics. Several times in the past few years, the "Wanted" column in *Good Old Days* magazine has included requests for the words to the song *I'm Tying the Leaves So They Won't Come Down.*

During the first decade of the 20th century, the lyrics and music were well known. Sheet music and phonograph recordings brought wide appeal to this popular number prior to the Great War. Decades later, many still recall *Tying the Leaves* and are drawn to the endearing essence of the story as portrayed through the meaningfully assembled words.

The original melody was composed by Fred Helf and the familiar lyrics were penned by E.S.S. "Erasmus" Huntington of Wallaceburg, Ontario, Canada. Helf and Hager Co. of New York City first copyrighted the popular song in 1907, and it was distributed by Hitland Music Publications. Soon the song hit the charts, achieving popularity in both the United States and Canada. More than 80 years later, the song's abated but continuing appeal is confirmed by those who still recall the touching story put to music.

The background of the story is not well known except in the area where the lyricist Erasmus Huntington lived. Wallaceburg is a western Ontario community in Kent County and is surrounded by two of the Great Lakes, Huron and Erie to the north and south respectively, and the smaller Lake St. Clair to the immediate southwest. The proximity of three large bodies of water subjects this area of Ontario to excessive periods of damp weather along with an abundance of humid air. As a result, bronchial ailments are common.

Erasmus Huntington was in love with a Wallaceburg girl, Ella Belle MacDonnell, sister of a prominent area shipbuilder. She suffered from the effects of the incessant dampness, and soon contracted a condition called bronchiectasis, a disorder of the bronchial tubes whereby excessive phlegm is accumulated, ultimately hindering normal breathing. Ella's condition worsened. Her medical confidant, Dr. George Mitchell, proclaimed that is was highly unlikely that his patient would survive the approaching autumn.

Huntington was distraught at the prospect of losing his beloved. He put his thoughts to words and developed the sentimental lyrics under the title *I'm Tying Down the Leaves So They Won't Fall Down.* When his lyrics were paired with Fred Helf's music, the combination resulted in the ballad's wide recognition as a popular song. The essence of the message centered around the doctor's prediction that Ella's life would end by the time the autumn leaves fell from the trees.

Huntington's lyrics offered a novel solution: "I've tied all the leaves fast upon the tree," thus prolonging the autumn season and preventing his loved one's death.

The story did have a somewhat happy ending, for Ella McDonnell did not die that autumn as predicted. However, she and Erasmus eventually drifted apart, and in soap-opera fashion, Ella eventually married her doctor's son, Harry Mitchell. Erasmus Huntington went his own way. Nevertheless, the legacy of their heartwarming love story has been revered through the beautiful words and music that became so well known to so many and are still recalled a generation later. ❖

I'm Tying the Leaves So They Won't Come Down

Words by E.S.S. Huntington
Music by J. Fred Helf

Playmates were they, girl and lad,
She's home today, lad feels sad,
Doctor who calls, whispers low,
"When the last autumn leaves fall,
Then she must go."
Lad with a tear climbs a tree.
"I'll keep her here," murmurs he.
Big man in blue sternly cries,
"What are you doing there?"
Lad replies,

Chorus:
*"I'm tying the leaves so they won't come
    down;*
So the wind won't blow them away,
*For the best little girl in the wide, wide
    world*
Is lying so ill today.
*Her young life must go when the last
    leaves fall;*
I'm fixing them fast so they'll stay.
*I'm tying the leaves so they won't come
    down,*
So Nellie won't go away."

Sad mother grieves, day by day,
Watching the leaves, hears boy say,
"You mustn't cry, for you see,
I have tied all the leaves fast upon
    the tree."
Doctor brings joy one glad day,
Mother tells boy Nell will stay.
Lad at girl's side cries with glee,
"That's what I said one day in the tree."

Repeat Chorus

When Your Old Wedding Ring Was New

By Eileen Higgins Driscoll

I was a little girl when Mother told me that *When Your Old Wedding Ring Was New* was her favorite song. She never told me why it was her favorite, but I guessed it many years later, after I was married.

Every time my parents had a wedding anniversary, our whole family celebrated. We didn't have much money because the country was still in the Depression in the 1930s. But we celebrated in our own way. It didn't cost much, but we loved it and it was fun.

There was always a special dinner, and we had a decorated cake with candles, just as if it were a birthday. All six of us kids would sing *Happy Anniversary to You* as loud as our little voices could sing. Then we would clap and each of us would give them both a big hug and a kiss.

We usually had a homemade present for them to open together. The best gift of all was always black-and-white snapshots. We took them with our Brownie camera and then carefully glued them into homemade frames we had made with our own little fingers.

It took us a whole week to make their anniversary cards. We helped the youngest kids make their cards and sign their names. The cards and pictures were all placed with great pride on the serving table, where they were displayed all week.

At some point during our celebration, Daddy would invariably get up from the head of the table and put his arm around Mother.

At some point during our celebration, Daddy would invariably get up from the head of the table and put his arm around Mother. He was a big man, but pretty much of a softie with us. His beautiful Irish tenor would fill the room when he sang *When Your Old Wedding Ring Was New* to Mama. She always seemed to have to blow her nose when the beautiful song ended. He was able to sing that special song to her 45 times before God took him.

We all benefited from this celebration of our parents' marriage. It gave us a deep feeling of family unity and strength. We were confident that none of us would ever be alone; we knew that we had each other for life.

Before we were married, my husband-to-be was invited to one of my parents' anniversary dinners in our home. We celebrated in the same way we had always done, sharing a dinner, presents and songs with each other. That evening before he went home, my fiancé, Jerry, promised me he would do the same for me when we were married. He was very impressed by the closeness and happiness the occasion brought to all of us.

He remembered his promise. We were alone on our first anniversary. We went to dinner in a neighborhood restaurant where a pianist was playing soft music for the dinner hour. We enjoyed a leisurely dinner together. Then I watched as Jerry got up and requested a song from the pianist. The man smiled up at him. When the song *When Your Old Wedding Ring Was New* began, my husband stood up, raised his wine glass and sang the moving words to me. We were alone in a crowd.

Everyone else in the restaurant was silent while they watched the two of us celebrate our anniversary. When the melody was finished, he leaned over, gave me a sweet kiss and sat down. All the people in the restaurant clapped for us.

Tears streaming down my cheeks, I knew then why Mama always had to blow her nose. I also figured out why it was her favorite song.

Wouldn't it be wonderful if all married couples started similar traditions that would be special to them and their children through the years? It might help some of them get over the bumps we all suffer during our lifetimes if more couples figured out a way to tell each other how much their love means to them. ❖

Cherishing the Memories by John Slobonik, House of White Birches nostalgia archives

When Your Old Wedding Ring Was New

When your old wedding ring
   was new
And the dreams that we
   dreamed came true
I remember with pride
When we stood side by side
What a beautiful picture
You made as my bride.
Now although silver crowns
   your hair,
I remember those gold ring-
   lets there …
Love's refrain still remains
As the day I changed your
   name
When your old wedding ring
   was new.

Faith & Inspiration

Chapter Three

*I*n younger days I was the music minister in our small country church, then served as lay pastor of another congregation for several years. I have always felt that the strength of our country lies in the strength of its families, the strength of its families lies in the strength of its churches, and the strength of our churches is bolstered by the songs of faith and inspiration lifted up to God.

"These see the works of the Lord, and his wonders in the deep. For he commandeth, and raiseth the stormy wind, which lifteth up the waves thereof." Every time I think of one of my favorite songs of faith and inspiration, *How Great Thou Art*, I think of those words from Psalm 107:24–25. A violent storm on a different continent inspired that well-loved hymn, penned by a man who, like me, was a pastor and editor.

It was on the rugged coast of Sweden in 1886 that the thunderstorm awed Carl Boberg, a Swedish minister who was also editor of a Christian newspaper and a member of the Swedish parliament. Boberg was struck by the contrast of the calm after the bluster and blow of the storm. The coastal water once again was placid, turned to thousands of diamonds in the returning sunlight. He heard "the birds sing sweetly in the trees," and their melody struck a chord in his heart.

The words he penned, set to the melody of a traditional Swedish folk song, would later be translated first into German and then Russian. Still, it languished in relative obscurity.

Then, in the 1930s, an English missionary to Czechoslovakia, Stuart Hine, heard the Russian version of the hymn. Boberg's original song consisted of the first verses and the chorus. Hine translated them to English and took them home with him at the outbreak of World War II. In 1948, while helping with refugees longing to return to their homelands, Hine added the fourth verse.

How Great Thou Art

O Lord my God, when I in awesome wonder
Consider all the worlds Thy hands have made,
I see the stars, I hear the rolling thunder,
Thy pow'r throughout the universe displayed!

When through the woods and forest glades
    I wander
And hear the birds sing sweetly in the trees,
When I look down from lofty mountain
    grandeur
And hear the brook and feel the gentle breeze,

And when I think that God, His Son not sparing,
Sent Him to die, I scarce can take it in—
That on the cross, my burden gladly bearing,
He bled and died to take away my sin!

When Christ shall come with shout of
    acclamation
And take me home, what joy shall fill my heart!
Then I shall bow in humble adoration
And there proclaim, my God,
    how great Thou art!

Chorus:
Then sings my soul, my Savior God, to Thee;
How great Thou art, how great Thou art!
Then sings my soul, my Savior God, to Thee;
How great Thou art, how great Thou art!

How Great Thou Art soared to popularity after extensive use in the Billy Graham Crusades. In 1974 it was selected as the favorite hymn among Americans in a poll conducted by the *Christian Herald*. It remains one of my favorite songs of faith and inspiration from the Good Old Days.

—*Ken Tate*

Grandpa Dodd and
The Old Rugged Cross

By Marta K. Dodd

When I used to think of Grandpa Dodd, I would picture him in his later years, sitting in a lawn chair behind my folks' southwestern Michigan farmhouse, puffing on his pipe, waiting for a somewhat unsuspecting relative or neighbor to come near. Then he would say, "Come sit down here for a minute."

He usually would get so busy talking as the minute stretched into many that the pipe would burn out from neglect. He might fire it up again, but soon it would be oxygen-deprived and the fire would fade once more.

My mental picture has him wearing his usual bib overalls, as we called them, and a striped engineer's hat perched on his head.

When I was a young child, I thought Grandpa was famous. He had, after all, played a violin in 1913 when the hymn *The Old Rugged Cross* was sung publicly in its entirety for the first time. The hymn's debut took place just a few miles down the road from our farm. I had to age a little to realize that it was the hymn, not Grandpa, that was famous.

Rev. George Bennard, a visiting evangelist, completed the hymn while visiting the First Methodist Episcopal Church in Pokagon, Mich., to help the pastor with some revival meetings. He sang the hymn in the

Rev. George Bennard composed The Old Rugged Cross *and more than 300 other hymns.*

church, playing his guitar. Then some local folks performed it from his penciled notes. We do not think that Grandpa was a member of the church when he added his violin to the musical mix of choir and organist in that performance. We think he was recruited to help out because he was known to play a pretty mean fiddle.

Soon after the hymn's debut, the church was sold and used as a storage barn for many years. It fell into serious disrepair, condition described in an article in *Good Old Days'* April 1990 issue. The hymn, however, went on to become an enduring international Christian favorite. In 1976, Rev. Bennard was named posthumously to the Gospel Music Association's Gospel Music Hall of Fame.

About a year after the hymn's debut, the bachelor fiddle player married, and another year or so later their first child was born. That child turned out to be my father.

Although I was a young adult when Grandpa Dodd died, I unfortunately did not discuss the hymn much with him. Over the last several years of my father's life, however, Pop and I talked about the church quite a bit. Pop always had the old church in mind, and at least once attempted to buy it so it could be restored. He occasionally bought a state lottery ticket and frequently said, "If I win, we'll restore the old

church." Sadly, it was not meant to happen in his lifetime.

Then, in 1998, a local couple bought the old church and donated it to their congregation, the current Pokagon United Methodist Church. They formed The Old Rugged Cross Foundation to lead efforts to restore the church as close as possible to its 1913 appearance and materials. The restored church will be available for weddings and other special services, and will include a small museum of church and local history. The Old Rugged Cross Foundation, a nondenominational volunteer 501(c)(3) organization, now owns the historic structure.

Soon after I became involved with the restoration effort, I had an opportunity to go inside the long-neglected church for the first time. I was very aware as I crossed the dusty threshold that I was walking where Grandpa had walked

Several participants in the 1913 public debut of the just-completed hymn The Old Rugged Cross *in Pokagon, Mich., gathered decades later for a commemorative photo. They included (from left) choir members Clara Virgil and Olive Marrs, organist Florence Jones, choir member Frank Virgil and violinist Arthur Dodd. Another choir member, William Thaldorf, was deceased. At the time of the hymn's debut, the three women were homemakers. Dodd operated a steam-powered grain-threshing business. Virgil worked for Michigan Central Railroad. Thaldorf's profession is not yet identified.*

Photo courtesy of Marta K. Dodd.

more than 85 years before, and where Pop had only dreamed of walking. What I was not aware of, until I stood at the front of the sanctuary, was what I would feel in that place. I began to talk aloud to "the Big Guy" as I fondly like to call God, and to my grandpa and Pop. I was making a commitment to do what I could to help bring the 1862 structure back.

I suddenly knew I was not alone, and that they were surrounding me with love and support. I took the only logical course. I burst into tears and sobbed as I finished my little speech to my small but important audience.

Since 1998, generous donations (mostly from individuals) have funded replacement of the deteriorated foundation that threatened the church with collapse. Temporary concrete piers now support the straightened, leveled structure. We have replaced decayed sill beams, braced the entire church, and installed a temporary new roof over the old one that allowed snow and rain into the sanctuary.

Our next challenge is to move the church onto the adjacent vacant lot and construct a new foundation and lower-level fellowship hall. Then we'll move the church back to its original location onto the new foundation. This work cannot take place until the funding is in hand.

Later phases of restoration also depend on funding. In the meantime, the original Old Rugged Cross Church, as we now call it, is a registered Michigan historic site.

The church is listed on the National Register of Historic Places, at the national level of historic significance.

The church also is an official project of Save America's Treasures, a partnership between the White House Millennium Council and the National Trust for Historic Preservation, dedicated to the preservation of our nation's irreplaceable historic and cultural treasures.

The newly created half-acre Old Rugged Cross Memorial Garden behind the old church creates a church-without-walls atmosphere as part of the Old Rugged Cross Historic Site.

Now, when I think of Grandpa Dodd and Pop, I know where they are, and I know they and the Big Guy are watching. And I know they all are waiting for us to restore this historic landmark so current and future generations can get on with the services that should be conducted there once again. ❖

For more information about the restoration, please write to The Old Rugged Cross Foundation at P.O. Box 41, Niles, MI 49120; (269) 683-4540; e-mail: orcf@aol.com; Web sites: www.the-oldruggedcross.org or www.theoldruggedcrossfoundation.org.

The original Old Rugged Cross Church as it appeared in 2002, with the temporary new roof installed. Photo courtesy of Marta K. Dodd.

The Old Rugged Cross

Words and music by George Bennard

On a hill far away stood an old
    rugged cross,
The emblem of suffering and shame;
And I love that old cross where the
    dearest and best
For a world of lost sinners was slain.

Chorus:
So I'll cherish the old rugged cross,
Till my trophies at last I lay down;
I will cling to the old rugged cross,
And exchange it some day for a crown.

Oh, that old rugged cross, so despised
    by the world,
Has a wondrous attraction for me;
For the dear Lamb of God left His
    glory above
To bear it to dark Calvary.

In the old rugged cross, stained with
    blood so divine,
A wondrous beauty I see;
For 'twas on that old cross Jesus
    suffered and died
To pardon and sanctify me.

To the old rugged cross I will ever
    be true,
Its shame and reproach gladly bear;
Then He'll call me some day to my
    home far away,
Where His glory forever I'll share.

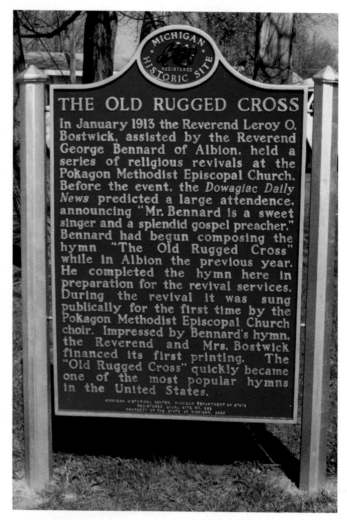

The Michigan historical marker near the original Old Rugged Cross Church was dedicated in April 2000.
Photo courtesy of Marta K. Dodd.

Mother's Favorite Hymn

By Lois Pinkerton Fritz

DICK SARGENT

It was twilight time as I sat down at the organ in the homestead to relax and play some of the old-fashioned hymns that Mother always loved. A tear slid down my cheek as I played *When the Roll Is Called Up Yonder*, for this was her favorite.

My mother, Sarah Irene Miller, had been a schoolteacher prior to her marriage to my dad during the Great Depression. After their marriage, they built a home in the little village of New Mahoning, Pa. She became a housewife and the mother of four children, of whom I was the eldest.

Cheerfully she'd go about her household chores—washing, ironing, canning, cleaning, sewing, cooking and baking. She baked wonderful homemade bread and cinnamon buns, not to mention delicious cakes and pies. She was well versed in this culinary art. As she worked, she hummed or sang many hymns she had known since childhood—and she always seemed to include her favorite.

Besides her household duties, she lovingly cared for her four children, who were born about two years apart. She was a loving mother who was always there to wipe away our tears and encourage us with these words from the Holy Bible: "This is the day which the LORD hath made; we will rejoice and be glad in it."

We were a singing family, and Mother was our inspiration. For many years, Daddy, my sister and one brother sang in the church choir while I played the organ. My older brother took the offering and Mother sang from her hymnal in the church pew.

I thank the Lord every night in my bedtime prayers that He gave us godly parents who raised us in the fear and admonition of the Lord. Church was our second home where we often sang beautiful hymns like *When the Roll Is Called Up Yonder*.

At the age of 96, Mother broke her hip. After surgery and brief rehab, we brought her back to her home where we cared for her until her final home going. In those days I often set up my portable electric keyboard and played the hymns she knew and loved. We'd sing like old times, for she remembered many of the words to these hymns, especially her favorite.

Having fulfilled her purpose here on earth, she was called home by God at the age of 99. At the home-going service, the minister used her favorite hymn. As I listened intently, I fully realized what an impact this hymn with its spiritual message and beautiful melody had had on my life, just as it had had on hers.

It's my prayer that when the roll is called up yonder, all the family will be there so that the family circle will be unbroken. In the meantime, I know Mother and her favorite hymn will continue to have a great influence on my life. ❖

When the Roll Is Called Up Yonder

Words and music by James M. Black

When the trumpet of the Lord shall sound, and
 time shall be no more,
And the morning breaks eternal
 bright and fair;
When the saved of earth shall gather over on the
 other shore,
And the roll is called up yonder, I'll be there.

Chorus:
When the roll is called up yonder,
When the roll is called up yonder,
When the roll is called up yonder,
When the roll is called up yonder I'll be there!

On that bright and cloudless morning when the
 dead in Christ shall rise,
And the glory of His resurrection share;
When His chosen ones shall gather to their
 home beyond the skies,
And the roll is called up yonder, I'll be there.

Let us labor for the Master from the dawn till
 setting sun,
Let us talk of all His wondrous love and care;
Then when all of life is over and our work on
 earth is done,
And the roll is called up yonder, I'll be there.

Is My Light Shining?

By Ann Casper as told to Jeannie Moore

In the Studebaker that my father owned, on Sundays we would take a drive around the countryside. My mother would sing songs and ask us to join her. One of my favorites was *This Little Light of Mine*. Those Sunday drives and my mother's music became a part of the way I viewed life.

Often when faced with a decision—whether it was to join a friend who was asking me to double-date, or to just take part in the simplest of activities—I asked myself, *Is my light shining?*

If I was tempted to make the wrong decision, I would remember my mother's song. Her music shaped my life and decisions as a teenager. I can remember a boy asking me to go to a dance with him, but he did not want to come pick me up. I knew this was against my parents' rule, but I really wanted to go to the dance. Finally I made the decision that living according to my parents' traditions were more important to me.

There have been times when I have been tempted to cheat a little on selling vegetables or other produce, but I remembered that my mother always told me to be completely honest, regardless of the situation, and to let my light shine. My mother often told me that being honest would reward my life in other ways. This has been true.

My husband and I were working on a ranch when the ranch manager asked us to overlook different cows that were not branded as ours. My husband and I knew the rancher was not totally honest and had been stealing cattle. The boss made it clear that if we did not lie for him we would be permanently out of work for him.

But my husband and I quit the ranch because the actions of the boss did not fit our standards of *This Little Light of Mine*. We were not sure how we would survive that winter, and Christmas was approaching. We knew we had to leave the situation to a higher power.

A couple of days before Christmas, there was a knock on the door. When we answered, the man at the door asked, "Is this the Casper house?"

"Yes. What can we do for you?"

"I have a Christmas box for you. May we bring it in?"

It was a Christmas box from the First Assembly of God church in Nowata, Okla. In it were several cans of food, a turkey, several wrapped presents and other items. This happened more than 50 years ago, and today, my church continues to try to help those in need.

I still remember my mother singing as we drove around the country in our old Studebaker. When my children were born in the late 1940s and early '50s, I continued the tradition of driving in the country and singing to my children. My mother's songs have made a difference in my life. I hope those songs and traditions continue to reflect the decisions my children make. ❖

This Little Light of Mine

By V.O. Fosset

This little light of mine, yes,
    I'm gonna let it shine;
This little light of mine, yes,
    I'm gonna let it shine;
Let it shine, let it shine, let it shine.

Hide it under a bushel? No!
    I'm gonna let it shine.
Hide it under a bushel? No!
    I'm gonna let it shine …
Let it shine, let it shine, let it shine.

Won't let Satan blow it out,
    I'm gonna let it shine;
Won't let Satan blow it out,
    I'm gonna let it shine;
Let it shine, let it shine, let it shine.

Let it shine till Jesus comes,
    I'm gonna let it shine;
Let it shine till Jesus comes,
    I'm gonna let it shine;
Let it shine, let it shine, let it shine.

O Holy Night

By Edna Staples

When I taught a special-education class back in the 1940s, I sent my students, ages 8–16, out to music each morning. Among my students was a 15-year-old girl who had a beautiful voice. Miss Wilson, the music teacher, should have been familiar with Gail's voice by now. She had been teaching the class for three months and was planning a Christmas program.

One morning after the class, Miss Wilson knocked on my door. She was rather excited. "Did you know Gail has an opera star voice? I heard her sing this morning. She has always sat in the back row and did not sing very loud."

"I have heard people say she has a beautiful voice," I said, "but she can hardly read. She also has a problem with her eyes."

"Will you teach her to read the Christmas songs if I teach her to sing them?" Miss Wilson asked.

"I certainly will," I said. The next day I added an extra reading class to Gail's schedule. Miss Wilson stayed after school to play the piano and listen to Gail sing. Gail was very cooperative, and so were her father and stepmother. By Christmas she had learned several carols.

The big night of the Christmas program finally arrived. The gym was crowded. After several grades had performed, Gail's solo was announced and she walked confidently across the stage.

The big night of the Christmas program finally arrived. The gym was crowded. Miss Wilson was at the piano; I sat nearby. Gail, in a pretty long dress made by her stepmother and a neat hairdo, was ready for the performance. After several grades had performed, Gail's solo was announced and she walked confidently across the stage.

Miss Wilson played the introduction to *O Holy Night*. The crowd grew very still as Gail's voice rang out: "O holy night, the stars are brightly shining." We were transported from the high school gym to a night far away, the night of our dear Savior's birth.

Some people, good singers, wiped their eyes. When she sang "Fall on your knees," we felt like doing just that.

When the song ended there was a hush before the applause. Gail did an encore and after the program she received lots of hugs and congratulations.

She became a very good reader. Although she never did become an opera singer, she sang in the church choir and school programs. She married young and raised four children, one of whom became a lawyer. *O Holy Night* became a turning point in her life. ❖

O Holy Night

By Adolphe Adam

O holy night! The stars are brightly shining,
It is the night of the dear Savior's birth;
Long lay the world in sin and error pining,
Till He appeared and the soul felt its worth.
A thrill of hope the weary world rejoices,
For yonder breaks a new and glorious morn;
Fall on your knees, Oh hear the angel voices!
O night divine, O night when Christ
  was born!
O night divine, O holy night,
  O night divine!

Led by the light of faith serenely beaming,
With glowing hearts by His cradle we stand;
So led by light of a star sweetly gleaming,
Here came the wise men from Orient land.
The King of Kings lay thus in lowly manger,
In all our trials born to be our friend;
He knows our need to our weakness is
  no stranger.
Behold your King, before Him lowly bend!
Behold your King, before Him lowly bend!

Truly He taught us to love one another;
His law is love, and His gospel is peace;
Chains shall He break, for the slave
  is our brother,
And in His name all oppression shall cease.

Sweet hymns of joy in grateful chorus
  raise we,
Let all within us praise His holy name;
Christ is the Lord Oh, praise His name
  forever!
His pow'r and glory evermore proclaim!
His pow'r and glory evermore proclaim!

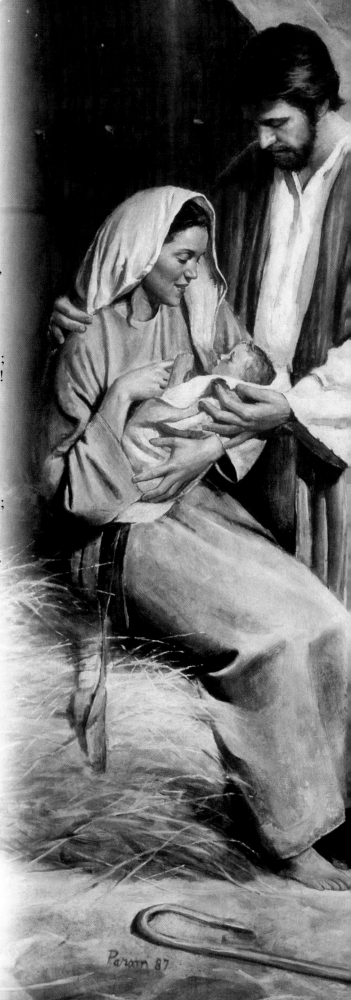

Live in the Sunshine!

By Glen Herndon

Mother never worried. She had two potent antidotes to what she called "the poison of worry."

First, she turned to her God in silent prayer, if only for a moment. I learned early on that when her eyes were closed, she was probably praying, and I would keep quiet.

Second, she used her beautiful alto voice to softly sing one of the old songs she had learned at her daddy's knee or—more likely—a hymn. She knew ever so many of them, and she passed them on to me. It is a legacy I treasure!

The hymn that seemed to mean the most to her was *Farther Along (We'll Know More About It)*.

I remember it so well, for I was a little boy at her elbow while she went about her chores when we were living in a humble clapboard house out in the middle of the oil fields south of Seminole, Okla., back in the early 1930s. With no neighbors nearby, no radio, not one musical instrument in the house, and with music welling up from her soul, she turned to her voice. "Cheer up, my brother! Live in the sunshine! We'll understand it all by 'n' by." And if she saw me with a glum look on my face, she was apt to tickle me—just a little—in the ribs!

"There is no room for doom and gloom, Doodle! Cheer up!"

She did her best against the odds of the times to make a happy home for all of us. She and Dad encouraged us boys to face the Depression and fight along with them, so we certainly could still have a good life even though lots of bad things came our way. Truly, we never had a hungry day, and Mother was noted for setting a groaning table.

On the other hand, there were a good number of people my folks talked about who engaged in illegal bootlegging, and stealing gas from the oil company's refinery. Mother and Dad often mentioned all the bank robberies by desperadoes of the day. Thinking about it, Mother would sing, "Tempted and tried, we're oft' made to wonder why it should be that all

the day long, while there are others living about us, never molested, doing the wrong."

One day her faith was put to a harsh test indeed. That was the day when Dad came home from work early, suffering with a migraine headache. She sat out on the lawn with him and put cold cloths on his forehead and motioned for me to be quiet. But I had to ask, "What's wrong with my daddy?"

"Daddy lost his job today," she whispered. "The oil company says the boom here is over, and they don't need him anymore."

Through his pain, Dad said, "It probably means we will have to move."

Mother replied, "Oh, Earl, we've done that so many times before! What if we do? Maybe we'll find things better at the new place!"

And in truth, our move was better for us all. Dad found work in new oil fields a little south of where we were, near Fittstown. Our move took place in early fall. We took our dogs, our cow, Daisy, and Mother's stores of canned goods, and before winter, we settled in a rented two-story farm home that also had a spacious attic where I could play with new friends on rainy days. It was one of those Victorian houses with lots of gingerbread decorations and lightning rods, reaching their spikes to the sky. Around it there were 500 acres and a creek to explore! I certainly liked it a lot better!

Mother really enjoyed our much-upgraded living conditions. She marveled at how God was opening doors for us.

One morning she stood in the large kitchen, frying up some of Dad's home-cured bacon and some eggs on the old cast-iron wood stove. Sunshine streamed in the window. I don't think she even noticed me, but I heard her familiar voice singing, "'Cheer up, my brother, live in the sunshine, We'll understand it all by 'n' by. Farther along we'll know more about it …' Why, Doodle, I didn't see you there! Come on and have some breakfast. Isn't this a day to thank God for?" ❖

Farther Along

Words and music by W.B. Stevens

Tempted and tried we're oft' made to wonder
Why it should be thus all the day long,
While there are others living about us,
Never molested, though in the wrong.

Chorus:
Farther along we'll know more about it,
Farther along we'll understand why;
Cheer up, my brother, live in the sunshine,
We'll understand it all by and by.

When death has come and taken our loved ones,
It leaves our home so lonely and drear;
Then do we wonder why others prosper,
Living so wicked, year after year.

Often I wonder why I must journey
Over a road so rugged and steep;
While there are others living in comfort,
While with the lost I labor and weep.

"Faithful till death," said our loving Master,
A few more days to labor and wait;
Toils of the road will then seem as nothing,
As we sweep through the beautiful gate.

When we see Jesus coming in glory,
When He comes from His home in the sky,
Then we shall meet Him in that
    bright mansion,
We'll understand it, all by and by.

My Brother's Mistake

By Ferne Smith Nee

One Sunday morning in 1939, church bells were ringing in our neighborhood, but I would not be going to church. Chronic bronchitis had me coughing day and night. I ached all over and needed to sleep.

Two hours later I heard Mother, Dad and Jay come into the house. My brother was in first grade, just learning to read. He bounced on my bed, beaming with excitement, and exclaimed, "You shoulda been there, Ferne! We sang a song about you in church. Here, I wrote the number on my paper." He pulled his Sunday school leaflet out of his coat pocket, then ran to get the hymnal from the piano. He found the page and slowly began to read:

"Beneath the cross of Jesus I Ferne would take my stand. …"

I couldn't believe my ears! I sat up, took the book and saw, "Beneath the cross of Jesus I fain would take my stand."

Jay was so little. I was the big sister, age 12. I couldn't embarrass him after he followed the words and tried to sing in church, and so I accepted his version of the hymn text. Mother and Dad went along with my request to use his word, just until he was older and found his mistake.

Music was a vital part of our lives. Dad was song leader at church. He sang in a male quartet and directed the community male chorus in Northampton, Pa. Mother accompanied these groups and played organ and piano at church.

I never owned an alarm clock because Mother woke me each day by playing hymns. My room was above the living room and the piano. After the fain/Ferne Sunday, she added "my" song to her repertoire. She loved the tune and especially the words. I sang along every time I heard it played.

> *Two hours later I heard Mother, Dad and Jay come into the house. My brother was in first grade, just learning to read. He bounced on my bed, beaming with excitement, and exclaimed, "We sang a song about you in church."*

After several weeks Mother said, "I'm glad you like the hymn Jay found for you. I would be even happier if you made the song truly yours." I thought I knew what she meant, but I asked her to help me understand how I could "take my stand" with Jesus.

My song became one of Mother's favorites. Our shared faith strengthened our relationship, and we worked together in music and children's ministry until she died in 1954.

Post-1980 hymnals have changed the first phrase of the hymn to "Beneath the cross of Jesus I gladly take my stand." The words may be different, but I continue to sing it in my heart the way my 6-year-old brother read it—personalized just for me. It wasn't a mistake at all. ❖

Beneath the Cross of Jesus

Words by Elizabeth C. Clephane
Music by Frederick C. Maker

Beneath the cross of Jesus I fain would take
my stand,
The shadow of a mighty rock within a
weary land;
A home within the wilderness, a rest upon
the way,
From the burning of the noontide heat, and
the burden of the day.

Upon that cross of Jesus mine eye at times
can see
The very dying form of One Who suffered
there for me;
And from my smitten heart with tears two
wonders I confess—
The wonders of His glorious love and my
unworthiness.

I take, O cross, thy shadow for my abiding
place;
I ask no other sunshine than the sunshine
of His face;

Content to let the world go by, to know no gain
nor loss,
My sinful self my only shame, my glory all
the cross.

O safe and happy shelter, O refuge tried
and sweet,
O trysting place where Heaven's love and
Heaven's justice meet!
As to the holy patriarch that wondrous dream
was given,
So seems my Savior's cross to me, a ladder
up to heaven.

There lies beneath its shadow but on the further side
The darkness of an awful grave that gapes both
deep and wide
And there between us stands the cross, two
outstretched arms to save,
A watchman set to guard the way from that
eternal grave.

1937 *The Household*, House of White Birches nostalgia archives

Life's Railway

By Allen H. Benton

I was born in 1921 on a small farm in central New York. My early years spanned the Great Depression, a time of falling prices for farm products and general unemployment across the nation. A popular song of the time went, "Eleven-cent cotton and 40-cent meat, how in the world can a poor man eat?"

We never lacked for food since we raised most of it right there on our farm. The few staples that we needed to purchase from the neighborhood grocery were paid for with eggs; cash was an almost absent commodity in our lives. Whatever money came in when crops were sold went to pay off the mortgage on our farm or the property taxes, which kept us from being displaced.

Though my parents were deeply religious, our poverty precluded active church membership for them. Much of the time we had no automobile in which we might have driven to church. My brother and I, however, could walk a half-mile or so to a corner where we could catch a ride with a neighbor, so we were brought up in the church from early childhood.

Mother had a pleasant soprano voice and was blessed with a musical talent that she often used in songs of praise. So far as I know, she never had any music lessons, but she could hear a song somewhere, then go home, sit down at the old piano in the parlor and pick out the tune, playing the melody with her right hand and the appropriate chords with her left.

During her few idle moments as a farm wife, Mother would often sit down to play and sing her favorite songs. Some were popular songs of the day, such as *Among My Souvenirs*, which I still hear on the radio occasionally. Others were old songs from her childhood during the Gay Nineties (that's the 1890s), comic songs like *McSorley's Most Beautiful Twins* or sentimental songs like *Seeing Nellie Home*. More often than not, though, she would sing a hymn. I associate

Old Ironsides by Jay Killian, House of White Birches nostalgia archives

many of those old hymns so closely with our little country church that I am not sure which ones I learned there and which ones I learned from Mother.

There is one song, though, which I never heard sung in church, but it was one of Mother's favorites. I was sure that no one else remembered it, but a few years ago, the organist in our church asked me if I had the words and music to that song. By chance, I had an old hymnbook that included it, so I gave it to him. Now he often plays it during the prelude before the service, though I have yet to hear it actually sung by our choir and congregation.

Not long ago, I was watching a television movie in which a male quartet sang at the funeral of an old friend, and to my surprise, I recognized the song they were singing as the old hymn that Mother used to sing. "Life is like a mountain railroad," she would sing, "with an engineer that's brave." Then it all came back to me in a flash—Mother sitting at the old piano, her long, dark hair done up in a bun that shifted precariously as she sang and nodded her head in time to the music. As I listened to the male quartet, it was my mother's voice I heard, and I could feel the tears close behind my eyelids as the song continued.

During the many years since I learned this song from Mother, there have been occasions when it was hard for me to "keep my eye upon the rail," and equally hard to surrender my hold on the throttle to a hand other than mine. But then the words of this song would pass through my mind, and I found its ancient promise both stirring and reassuring. I'm sure that this song has meant just as much to me as it did to Mother throughout her life. ❖

Life's Railway to Heaven

Words by M.E. Abbey
Music by Charlie D. Tillman

Life is like a mountain railroad,
With an engineer that's brave;
We must make the run successful,
From the cradle to the grave;
Watch the curves, the fills, the tunnels;
Never falter, never quail;
Keep your hand upon the throttle,
And your eye upon the rail.

Chorus:
Blessed Savior, Thou wilt guide us,
Till we reach that blissful shore
Where the angels wait to join us
In Thy praise forevermore.

You will roll up grades of trial;
You will cross the bridge of strife;
See that Christ is your conductor
On this lightning train of life;
Always mindful of obstruction,

Do your duty, never fail;
Keep your hand upon the throttle,
And your eye upon the rail.

You will often find obstructions;
Look for storms of wind and rain;
On a fill, or curve, or trestle,
They will almost ditch your train;
Put your trust alone in Jesus;
Never falter, never fail;
Keep your hand upon the throttle,
And your eye upon the rail.
As you roll across the trestle,
Spanning Jordan's swelling tide,
You behold the Union Depot
Into which your train will glide;
There you'll meet the Superintendent,
God the Father, God the Son,
With the hearty, joyous plaudit,
"Weary pilgrim, welcome home!"

A Song of
Faith & Hope

By Verla A. Moot

Growing up in the foothills of the Ozark Mountains of southwest Missouri during the 1930s, music was as integral a part of my family's lifestyle as were eating and sleeping. My sister, Beatrice, who was four years older than I, played the pump organ, and I learned to play the guitar when I was only 11. I later studied organ and taught music lessons. Both of my younger brothers played guitars and sang. Daddy sometimes played the harmonica with us. On summer evenings we would sit outside on the grass and play and sing until bedtime. In the winter we gathered around the pump organ in our small front room and made music and sang.

As deeply ingrained into our way of life as music was the custom of lending a helping hand to a neighbor or friend in times of sickness and death. Daddy was known for always sitting up with the sick and digging graves when a death occurred in our rural community. Few people had money to go to the hospital in the years of the Great Depression. Mama was asked to help deliver babies and sing at funerals. There wasn't anyone in the entire community that had a lovelier voice or a sweeter disposition than Mama.

How vividly I remember the summer that I was 5 years old. A close neighbor whom we called Grandma Holbrook died, and Mama was asked to sing. I begged to stay home with a neighbor girl and my older sister and brother, but Mama said I was too little.

It was a sweltering afternoon in the middle of August. The service was held under a shade tree in the front yard. The funeral director brought folding chairs and placed them under the tree. Mama was seated behind the casket to the left of the minister. I was standing beside her. I stood with downcast eyes so I wouldn't have to look at the casket.

When Mama started to sing, she caught my attention immediately, for I had never heard this song before. The tempo was faster and the melody was beautiful. I looked up at Mama. Her face was not sad, and her eyes were cast slightly upward as if she was beholding something that was invisible to me.

My childish mind could not understand all the meaning of the words of the song *No Disappointment in Heaven*. I only knew that I loved Mama's song and I wanted to hear her sing it again. Even at the tender age of 5, I understood that life is made up of both sunshine and shadows. What had been shadows to me had suddenly turned to sunshine as Mama sang her song.

When I started to school that fall, I did not go with Mama as often, but I never stopped asking her to sing *No Disappointment in Heaven* each time we sang. By the time I was 10, Mama's song had become my song as well. I sang it at church and in neighbors' homes whenever I was asked. By the me Beatrice and I reached our teenage years, we were also singing for funerals. It was not my favorite place to sing, but we never thought of refusing. If the family of the deceased did not request a special song, we chose our own. Beatrice's favorite was *Beautiful Isle of Somewhere*. I always wanted to sing Mama's song.

Once we were asked to sing at the funeral of an elderly lady who had not lived in our community very long. After the funeral, her daughter from New York came up and handed us a sealed envelope. We opened it at home and to our surprise, it contained a note of thanks with $15 in it. Such a thing was unheard of in the Ozarks at that time, at least in our rural area.

Although $15 seemed like a fortune, our mother told us we should send it back to the lady. Mama admonished us, saying, "Your talents were given to you by God, and you must never expect pay for singing at a neighbor's funeral."

During World War II, I worked on an Army post and married a soldier from Chicago. Following the war, we moved back to the Windy City. Although my lifestyle was vastly changed as wife, mother and homemaker, I still sang Mama's beautiful song when the occasion arose. When my son was in college and my daughter in her last year of high school, I was asked to help start a department of pastoral care at a nearby 600-bed hospital. I felt it best to go to work to help fill the void in my life while my children were away at college. I became a chaplain and coordinator of interfaith pastoral care.

The next 11 years of my life, when I was working as a chaplain—eight years in the hospital and three in a nursing home—were both the most rewarding and the most difficult. One of the hospital floors to which I was assigned was a cancer floor. I never learned the fine art of being both compassionate and caring without sometimes caring too deeply.

I remember one of the first cancer patients to whom I was assigned. She was a lady around my age. I talked with her for hours about life after death. She was so anxious and filled with countless questions. The end was drawing near for her, and I wasn't sure she had found peace of mind.

One day I went into her room and she lay facing the wall. I softly spoke her name as I bent over her hospital bed. She turned and grabbed my hand, pleading with me to tell her more about eternal life. Pulling a chair close to her bed, I sat down and held her hand. I wanted so much to ease her apprehension. Her eyes were filled with fear and her hand felt cold, although it was summertime.

My mind rapidly searched for scripture verses on death and dying, but I was at a loss for words. Then I suddenly thought of the peace that had swept over a small girl's heart when Mama sang her song so long ago. Trying to keep a sob out of my voice, I softly began to sing:

"There's no disappointment in heaven,
No weariness, sorrow or pain,
No hearts that are bleeding and broken,
No song with a minor refrain;
The clouds of our earthly horizon
Will never appear in the sky;
For all will be sunshine and gladness,
With never a cloud in the sky."

The patient took one long, deep breath and her hand went limp in mine. I gently laid her hand across her chest and rang for the nurse. In the words of the poet, I knew she had safely made the journey across the "dark river of death."

While waiting for the nurse to come, although I knew that the patient was beyond the sound of my voice, I quietly sang the last two triumphant lines of the third verse, perhaps to bring comfort to my own heart: "Immortal, we will stand in His likeness, the stars and the sun to outshine."

When searching for words to soothe the patients' pain and fears, Mama's song became one of the instruments of ministry I often used. I had read thousands of pages of theology, but even as the words of the song had helped me when I was a child, they are now a solid foundation to which my faith and hope are still anchored.

My mother's beautiful voice has been silenced here on earth for the past 20 years, but it still lives on in my heart. I seldom hear the song sung anymore. Far too many of the songs of faith are being replaced by contemporary Christian music, but they can never surpass the songs my mother sang in those Good Old Days of long ago. ❖

No Disappointment In Heaven

Words and music by Frederick M. Lehman
Harmony by Claudia Lehman Mays

There's no disappointment in heaven,
No weariness, sorrow or pain;
No hearts that are bleeding and broken,
No song with a minor refrain.
The clouds of our earthly horizon
Will never appear in the sky;
For all will be sunshine and gladness,
With never a sob or a sigh.

Chorus:
I'm bound for that beautiful city
My Lord has prepared for His own;
Where all the redeemed of all ages
Sing "Glory!" around the white throne;
Sometimes I grow homesick for heaven,
And the glories I there shall behold;
What a joy that will be when my Savior I see,
In that beautiful city of gold!

We'll never pay rent for our mansion,
The taxes will never come due;
Our garments will never grow threadbare,
But always be fadeless and new;
We'll never be hungry nor thirsty,
Nor languish in poverty there,
For all the rich bounties of heaven
His sanctified children will share.

There'll never be crepe on the doorknob,
No funeral train in the sky;
No graves on the hillside of glory,
For there we shall nevermore die.
The old will be young there forever,
Transformed in a moment of time;
Immortal we'll stand in His likeness,
The stars and the sun to outshine.

Where We'll Never Grow Old

By Opal Chadwick Blaylock

Mama was born in Van Buren County, Ark., on June 21, 1892. Her parents, Alva Shull and Charlie Roberts, named her Leah Elizabeth, but as mountain folks sometimes did, they flattened it a tad and called her Lear.

Mama's likes and dislikes were not influenced by radio, television or books. Friends and family simply passed on the things they knew and loved. Mama's taste in music was shaped by the hymns of the church and the folk songs her family sang while sitting on the porch. Mostly these songs were sung without benefit of musical instruments.

On rare occasions a stringed instrument would be played. Hand clapping or foot tapping kept the rhythm. Mama didn't sing; she hummed. Oh, she knew the words to the tunes, but she liked to hum. She did it while she worked in her vegetable garden, gathered eggs from the henhouse and fed her chickens. Sometimes she hummed while she pedaled the old treadle sewing machine while she made our clothes. She kept the rhythm smooth and steady.

I learned the words by heart. The hope of a better day was clear and comforting.

Mama liked to hear music and singing, but she didn't like what she called "that foolish stuff." It always amused us when she said, "They make up a song about anything and then sing it."

Life in her early years was very hard. The folk songs were sad because they were often about the death of a child or other loved ones. They were sung in a lonesome wail. Many of the songs were hopeless accounts of a life event. It was their sad lyrics that most likely gave Mama her appreciation of songs about heaven.

The tune she hummed most often was *Where We'll Never Grow Old* by James C. Moore. When I was a young girl with only a few piano lessons behind me, she asked when I would be able to play songs from the hymnbook. Shortly after that I began to pick out a few of her favorite hymns, one note at a time, with my right hand. Among the first was *Where We'll Never Grow Old.* "Read the words," she would say. "Don't get lost in just playing the song."

I learned the words by heart. The hope of a better day was clear and comforting. I began to understand why the words meant so much to her, and I embraced the message for myself.

My father, Walter Chadwick, the only man Mama ever kissed, died in January 1947. My brother was in the Army, stationed in

ermany. My oldest sister had married her return-
g soldier boyfriend just a few days before. I
as 15 years old and the only child left at home.
Iama's health was deteriorating and her heart was
heavy. She sat for days, her hands folded in her
p. I had seldom seen her hands so idle.

Then, one spring day, I came home from
hool to find Mama working on her quilt blocks—
d though it was barely audible, she was hum-
ing. I started singing the last verse: "When our
ork here is done and our life crown is won, and
ir troubles and trials are o'er; all our sorrow will
d …" Then, to my surprise, Mama joined in and
ng the last line: "… and our voices will blend
ith the loved ones who've gone on before."

Mama experienced the most devastating thing
a mother can face, not once but twice in her life.
As a young mother she lost her second daughter,
Beulah Irene, at 6 weeks. Then, when Mama was
80 years old, her daughter Joyce was killed in an
auto accident a few minutes after leaving Mama's
house. Mama never recovered from that loss. She
lived for three more years, longing for that place
where "all sorrow will end."

When Mama died in October 1975, a simple
four-part harmony was played on an old upright
piano while a small choir sang her song. Age-
less now, and painless, Mama could join Daddy
and the angels, singing "Happy praises to the
king," and she'd never have to stop! ❖

Where We'll Never Grow Old

Words and music by James C. Moore

have heard of a land on the faraway strand,
'is a beautiful home of the soul;
uilt by Jesus on high, there we never shall die,
'is a land where we'll never grow old.

horus:
ever grow old, never grow old,
* a land where we'll never grow old;*
ever grow old, never grow old,
* a land where we'll never grow old.*

 that beautiful home where we'll
   nevermore roam,
'e shall be in that sweet by and by;
appy praise to the King through eternity sing,
'is a land where we never shall die.

/hen our work here is done and our life
   crown is won,
nd our troubles and trials are o'er,
ll our sorrows will end, and our voices
   will blend,
/ith the loved ones who've gone on before.

YES! we have no bananas
BY
Frank Silver and
Irving Cohn
FRUITS
PUBLISHED BY
SKIDMORE MUSIC CO. Inc
MUSIC PUBLISHERS
NEW YORK
MADE IN U.S.A.
SELLING AGENTS
Shapiro, Bernstein & Co.
MUSIC
PUBLISHERS
COR. BROADWAY & 47th STREET
New York

Just for Fun

Chapter Four

When I was in primary grades in the small rock school atop a high hill in Hollister, Mo., Mrs. Bartholomew was our music teacher. Her primary responsibility was teaching high school choir and band classes, but once or twice a week the grade school children were treated to music class with Mrs. Bartholomew.

She taught us rhythm using sticks and tambourines, and pitch using her old upright piano. I later came to be a pretty good vocalist, and I give her the credit for putting up with my croaking as a youngster.

I have two main memories of those early music classes: fear and fun. Fear came from the imposing presence of that lady, who was short of stature but iron of will. She had a paddle with holes drilled in it that we kids came to call the "Swiss cheese paddle." We were sure she had the holes drilled in it to cut down wind resistance when applying it to the backside of an offender.

The fun came from Mrs. Bartholomew's selection of music. We sang the "Yo heave ho" of the *Volga Boat Song*, and the "knapsack on my back" of *The Happy Wanderer*.

But one of my favorites of those songs we sang just for fun was *YES! We Have No Bananas!* Its lyrics, written by Frank Silver and Irving Cohn in 1923, reminded me of the shopkeepers and merchants in nearby Branson. They might not have what you were looking for, but would be the last to admit it.

We kids loved singing those comical words, especially emphasizing the chorus:

Yes! We Have No Bananas!

There's a fruit store on our street.
It's run by a Greek,
And he keeps good things to eat,
But you should hear him speak
When you ask him anything
Never answers "no"

He just "yesses" you to death
And as he takes your dough
He tells you:

Chorus:
YES! We have no bananas!
We have no bananas today.
We've string beans and HON-ions,
Cab-BAH-ges and scallions
And all kinds of fruit and say—
We have an old fashioned to-MAH-to,
Long Island po-TAH-to.
But YES! We have no bananas!
We have no bananas today!

Bus'ness got so good with him
He wrote home to say
"Send me Pete and Nick and Jim,
I need help right away."
When he got them in the store
There was fun, you bet
Someone asked for "Sparrow-grass"
And then the whole quartette
All answered:

YES! We have no bananas!
We have no bananas today.
We've string beans and HON-ions,
Cab-BAH-ges and scallions
And all kinds of fruit and say—
We have an old fashioned to-MAH-to,
Long Island po-TAH-to.
But YES! We have no bananas!
We have no bananas today!

I lost track of Mrs. Bartholomew in later years, but if I could speak to her today, I would thank her for helping me develop a deep-rooted love of music. Those songs we sang just for fun will always make me smile as I remember her music room back in the Good Old Days.

—*Ken Tate*

Take Me Out To the Ball Game

By Eileen Higgins Driscoll

Every time I hear the song *Take Me Out to the Ball Game*, it takes me right back to my memories of Ebbets Field in Brooklyn, N.Y. It opened in 1913. We grew up and lived nearby during the 1930s–1950s. We loved many of the players on the Brooklyn Dodgers baseball team; they were our hometown heroes.

My first recollection of baseball was watching the kids on our block play stickball in the streets when I was about 6 years old. "Hey Tommy," they would yell, "you hit that ball just like Duke Snyder!" Tommy would laugh and yell back at them while he ran the bases. "Foul ball!" someone else would cry out—and the batter would throw the stick and hang his head. I don't think there ever was a bad game of stickball when we were growing up.

On many hot nights during the summer, my mother and father would sit outside on the back porch and listen to the ball game on the radio. Sometimes they tuned in to listen to Red Barber calling the plays in his soft, Southern accent. Sometimes they listened to Vin Scully broadcasting the game from Ebbets Field. Once in a while I heard them yelling, too. "He's safe on second!" "Another home run!" "The announcer just said that umpire needs glasses!"

Sometimes, if they let me stay up late, I would sit out on the porch and listen to the game with them. Mother would make homemade ice-cream sodas, putting cream soda in a tall glass with a little milk and vanilla ice cream. Boy, they were good! That memory always brings a smile to my heart.

All the kids in the neighborhood traded baseball cards that came with bubble gum. Duke was a better player than Pete Rizzo and Campanella so that became a two-for-one trade. Gil Hodges lived in our neighborhood. That made him a very special favorite. We walk very slowly past his house in hopes of catching a glimpse of him. Our parents had warned us not to bother him because that wasn't polite.

Mother sang *Take Me Out to the Ball Game* when she was alone in the kitchen or doing the dishes. Sometimes I would sing along. Then Dad got a good idea. One day Dad asked me, "How would you like to go to the ball game with Mother and me tomorrow afternoon?" Wow, what a treat for a 9-year-old kid!

We took the Flatbush Avenue trolley car to downtown Bedford Avenue. It was a thrill just to join the crowd waiting to buy an admission ticket. I think it cost a quarter in those days. The cement floor and the tunnel to the stands had a special smell; I think it was a mixture of people, grass, popped corn and hot dogs.

Dad bought a score card and taught me how to keep all the runs and strikes marked properly. I loved it. We sat up in the bleachers. When I looked down, the grass seemed greener than any other grass I had ever seen. The dirt on the baseball diamond was raked to perfection. The sun shone all around us and excitement filled the air.

Once we were all settled in our seats, Dad left us. But he was back in a few minutes, with a big smile and three hot dogs with sauerkraut and mustard all over them. I guarantee that you will never find a hot dog that tastes that good, no matter where you look.

Dad bought a score card and taught me how to keep all the runs and strikes marked properly. I loved it. We sat up in the bleachers. When I looked down, the grass seemed greener than any other grass I had ever seen. The dirt on the baseball diamond was raked to perfection.

The organ got the fans' attention. Then an announcer called out the lineup of players for the game. When the players ran out onto the field, the whoops and shouts and applause were wonderful. Then all fell quiet and we stood at attention, hands over our hearts, for our national anthem. Finally the game began.

During the seventh-inning stretch, Daddy disappeared again. He returned with another surprise: a box of Cracker Jack for each of us. Not only were there peanuts in each box, but also a prize at the bottom.

We all went home after the game tired and happy. It was always good if our team won, but if they didn't, that was OK, too. There was always next time. All of Brooklyn loved "dem Bums."

Brave Jackie Robinson and Branch Rickey broke the color barrier in 1947. Together they gave the world a lesson in civil rights. They both displayed a lot of courage and integrity to stand together for what they thought was right against great adversity.

When I grew older, my friends would go to the game with me. The man that was to be my husband worked as an usher there during his high school and college years. He told stories of how he would dust the seats carefully for the people in the box seats and always get a tip.

During the early 1950s we enjoyed a special treat. A friend of my husband's brought us into Ebbets Field on a press pass as guests. We were brought up to a private room that was used for the press people and their guests. We were served refreshments and met some of the reporters from the *Brooklyn Eagle* newspaper. Women reporters were scarce in those days.

Just before the game started, we were brought down to the press box where Waite Hoyt was announcing the game that day. He was busy giving the pregame chatter when we arrived. There he was, seated at a table overlooking the field. His TV audience could see him only from the waist up, and he was wearing a hat, sport jacket, shirt, tie—and boxer shorts. It was such a hot day that he had removed his slacks since no women were expected. He stammered a little and his face got red when he caught sight of me. I simply smiled and said in a low voice, "Don't worry. It's OK." He continued announcing and we all enjoyed the game.

Baseball taught me many things besides baseball: It taught me that teamwork makes everything easier in ball games and other aspects of life. You feel good all over when you sing. Family fun together keeps people close forever. It doesn't matter if

you don't always win if you play the game fair and do your best. Respect every person you meet, even if his skin happens to be a different color than yours. And always keep your pants on when out in public, even on a hot day.

But the biggest lesson of all was the knowledge that I happened to have the best mother and father in the whole wide world. ❖

Take Me Out to the Ball Game
By Jack Norworth

(**Editor's note:** Norworth wrote another version in 1908, but updated it in 1927.)

Nelly Kelly loved baseball games,
Knew the players, knew all their names,
You could see her there ev'ry day,
Shout "Hurray,"
When they'd play.
Her boyfriend by the name of Joe
Said, "To Coney Isle, dear, let's go,"
Then Nelly started to fret and pout,
And to him I heard her shout:

Chorus:
Take me out to the ball game.
Take me out with the crowd.
Buy me some peanuts and Cracker Jack.
I don't care if I never get back.
Let me root, root, root for the home team.
If they don't win it's a shame.
For it's one, two,
Three strikes you're out,
At the old ball game.

Nelly Kelly was sure some fan.
She would root just like any man.
Told the umpire he was wrong,
All along,
Good and strong.
When the score was just two to two,
Nelly Kelly knew what to do,
Just to cheer up the boys she knew,
She made the gang sing this song:

Repeat Chorus

Rudolph's Rise to Fame

By Gerald Ramey

*I*t was in the spring of 1939 that the sales manager of Montgomery Ward & Co. tired of buying crummy little nothings for Christmas giveaways. He called in advertising copywriter Robert L. May and assigned him to remedy the situation.

May thought about it for the next several weeks. The idea was to write a children's story booklet to hand out to Ward's shoppers during the Christmas season. He decided the hero of the story would be a reindeer different from Santa's other deer: a reindeer who could lead Santa's team and keep them on course during a very dark and foggy Christmas Eve; a reindeer with a large, bright red nose to light the way; sort of an "ugly duckling" who in the end would outshine them all. *Rudolph the Red-Nosed Reindeer* was the result.

May told the story all in a rhyme, and the result was given to shoppers in the form of an attractive, 32-page, softcover book illustrated by Denver Gillen. *Rudolph the Red-Nosed Reindeer* proved to be one of Ward's most popular promotional items.

Robert May received only a $300 bonus for his effort. But it didn't end there. In 1946, Ward's chairman, the late Sewell Avery, overrode objections of staff lawyers who wanted the copyright retained by the company. Avery decreed that Bob May should have the rights.

The hero of the story would be a reindeer different from Santa's other deer: a reindeer who could lead Santa's team and keep them on course during a very dark and foggy Christmas Eve.

The following year, a small Chicago children's book publisher, Maxton and Co., brought out a Rudolph edition that sold 100,000 copies in just two years. Then, in 1949, popular songwriter Johnny Marks saw a copy of *Rudolph* and it inspired him to write the song that became No. 1 on the *Hit Parade*—and it has been on the hit parade every Christmas season since.

Gene Autry recorded *Rudolph* against his will, but it

became one of his top-selling records. The story of *Rudolph the Red-Nosed Reindeer* has been made into movies and television cartoons. There are Rudolph clocks, radios, lamps, toys, games, cookie cutters, comic books and many other items starring the outcast reindeer with the glowing nose.

Robert May never said how much he made on royalties, but he did say it was a big help in the education of his six children and made it possible for him and his family to travel all over this country and to Europe.

But May continued working as a middle-management catalog editor. He said he was not a real genius like Walt Disney or Dr. Seuss, who could create supreme successes again and again.

He was under no delusion that something like Rudolph would ever happen to him again. Even so, wouldn't it be nice to have just one big success, like Robert L. May did?

So congratulations, Rudolph! May you lead Santa's sleigh for many years to come! ❖

Rudolph the Red-Nosed Reindeer

Words and music by Johnny Marks

You know Dasher and Dancer and
Prancer and Vixen,
Comet and Cupid and Donner and Blitzen,
But do you recall
The most famous reindeer of all?

Rudolph, the red-nosed reindeer
Had a very shiny nose
And if you ever saw it,
You would even say it glows.

All of the other reindeer
Used to laugh and call him names,
They never let poor Rudolph
Join in any reindeer games;

Then one foggy Christmas Eve,
Santa came to say:
"Rudolph, with your nose so bright,
Won't you guide my sleigh tonight?"

Then how the reindeer loved him
As they shouted out with glee:
"Rudolph the red-nosed reindeer,
You'll go down in history!"

Rudolph the Red-Nosed Reindeer *appeared in Montgomery Ward & Co. to lead Santa's sleigh (and Ward's cash registers) toward loads of Christmas cheer.*

Here Comes Santa Claus

By Gerald Ramey

Editor's note: Rudolph the Red-Nosed Reindeer *wasn't the last Christmas song Gene Autry had his hands in making famous. He co-wrote another Christmas favorite,* Here Comes Santa Claus *in 1947. Here are the words to that old favorite.*

Here Comes Santa Claus

*Words and music by Gene Autry
and Oakley Haldeman*

Here comes Santa Claus! Here comes
   Santa Claus!
Right down Santa Claus Lane!
Vixen and Blitzen and all his reindeer
Are pulling on the rein.
Bells are ringing, children singing
All is merry and bright.
Hang your stockings and say your pray'rs,
'Cause Santa Claus comes tonight.

Here comes Santa Claus! Here comes
   Santa Claus!
Right down Santa Claus Lane!
He's got a bag that is filled with toys
For the boys and girls again.
Hear those sleigh bells jingle jangle
What a beautiful sight
Jump in bed, cover up your head,
'Cause Santa Claus comes tonight.

Here comes Santa Claus! Here comes
   Santa Claus!
Right down Santa Claus Lane!
He doesn't care if you're rich or poor
For he loves you just the same.
Santa knows that we're God's children
That makes ev'rything right.

Here Comes Santa Claus © 1947
by Gene Autry Music Publishing
Inc., Hollywood, Calif.

Fill your hearts with a Christmas cheer,
'Cause Santa Claus comes tonight.

Here comes Santa Claus! Here comes
   Santa Claus!
Right down Santa Claus Lane!
He'll come around when the chimes ring out
Then it's Christmas morn again.
Peace on earth will come to all
If we just follow the light.
Let's give thanks to the Lord above,
'Cause Santa Claus comes tonight.

Yust Going Nuts!

By D.A. Guiliani

Who was Yogi Yorgesson? I have no idea, but this "Scandinavian" recorded a song in 1950 that swept the Midwest, the Upper Midwest, the Upper Peninsula (U.P.) of Michigan, Wisconsin, Minnesota and North Dakota, and attracted Scandinavians for mining, forestry and above all, dairy farming. Swedes, Norwegians and Danes came to the North Woods for opportunity. Lefse, lutefisk and music are found in the area still, and baby boomers and older folks here still grin over Yogi's songs. The big hit was a holiday tune called *I Yust Go Nuts at Christmas.*

The first 7-inch, 45-rpm record came out in 1949. Like today's CDs, 45s brought out recordings by unknowns. The 45s were easier to produce than the larger 78s, so opportunities abounded. Big-name record companies had scores more releases each year than they had with the larger, thicker records. Yogi was one of those on the Capitol label.

We had never had a 78-rpm Victrola (though my grandparents did), but my dad brought home one of those new, funny-looking record players that didn't have a top but did have a large cylinder in the center of the round base. Plug it in, turn a switch, and a record dropped from the top of the cylinder to the base, the arm moved from its narrow stand, and *voila*, music came out of the speaker! This sure was easier than all that handle winding. Wow, we were high-tech—except that in those days, we said "new-fangled," not "high-tech."

Dad had talked the record player seller into giving him a few records as a bonus. Dad chose

The first time I heard Yogi's Christmas song, I was puzzled. At age 8, I had to hear the words again and again. The "j" was pronounced as a "y": "just" was pronounced "yust," "join" was "yoin." Swedes and Norwegians knew that, but this Italian kid didn't catch it right away.

a Vaughn Monroe record and Yogi Yorgesson's Christmas song. Dad told us he chose it because the singer was a Swede; he had known some Swedes and they had been good singers.

Those of us who grew up in the U.P. don't need any speeches on diversity. Our copper and iron mines employed literally dozens of ethnic groups from many foreign lands. One copper company alone, Calumet & Hecla, subscribed to 16 European newspapers so the workers could keep in touch with events in "the old country."

In my hometown of Iron Mountain, we had Italians, Swedes, Norwegians, Finns, Bohemians, Croats, Germans, French-Canadians, Belgians, Lebanese and "Cousinjacks," the name for the English who had come from the Cornwall tin and copper mines seeking better wages.

On the north side of town were neighborhood grocery stores where English was seldom heard. There, Italian was the norm. Some Swedes ran our ice-skating rink. If they didn't want us kids in on a conversation, they just switched from English to Swedish.

As a youngster, I used to attend the annual Swede-Cousinjack baseball game at the East Side Athletic Association field. The teams came to the ballpark from downtown in a parade with floats and bands. During a game, treats were given to the Swedes' and Cousinjacks' kids. I might have been mostly Italian, but I had blond hair and blue eyes—a faint touch of German, compliments of my maternal grandfather. The men giving out the soda pop, popcorn and ice-cream cones assumed I was a Larson or Peterson or Anderson or Johnson. (Our city's skinny phone directory had a full page of listings for each of those names.) I never id I was a Swede, but being poor and sizing p the chance for a rare treat, I did nothing to let em know I wasn't. In the early 1950s, three eats in one afternoon was a fantasy—unless you ere at the annual Swede-Cousinjack game.

The first time I heard Yogi's Christmas song, was puzzled. At age 8, I had to hear the words gain and again. The "j" was pronounced as a y": "just" was pronounced "yust," "join" was yoin." Swedes and Norwegians knew that, but is Italian kid didn't catch it right away.

After listening several times, I realized that e song was truly funny—actually hilarious. ogi sang, "I look at nightgowns for my wife, all lack ones trimmed in red, but I don't know her ize and so she'll get the carpet sweeper instead." omebody named Uncle Louis gets into a fight vhile the radio is playing in the background with Gabriel Heatter saying "Peace on earth, every-ody." Those were clever, satirical lines.

It didn't hurt that we could rib my dad a it, seeing as his name was Louie. "It's a time or kids to flip their lids while the papa goes in ock." My dad laughed at those words.

The song also talks about the quiet after dinner: "Them relatives start swarming all over the yoint." That always hit home with me because our house was the gathering place for both sides of the family. My mom's sister and her husband stopped by, and my dad's sister and her husband came over, too, and they all had children. And our little house was full, "yust like that."

As I was growing up, through my adolescence and into young adulthood, we always played that song on Christmas Eve. We all laughed and sang along.

As an adult, I was a high school teacher in a girls' school. Students brought mountains of gifts for teachers at Christmas. My gift to the students was a break from economics. I told the girls the history of the U.P.—the ethnicity, thanks to the mining industry. Then I'd tell them to gather around the old record player on the table in the classroom, and I'd play *I Yust Go Nuts at Christmas* for them. "Play it again, play it again!" they'd cry. Their requests took me right back to our 1950 living room as they echoed my words to my dad: "Play it again!" Thanks, Yogi. ❖

I Yust Go Nuts at Christmas

Performed by Yogi Yorgesson

Editor's note**Editor's note:** *We were unable to determine the author or composer of this Christmas novelty song that was first released in 1939. We have done the best o reproduce the song s true to its original Scandinavian accent s possible.*

Oh! I yust go nuts at
    Christmas!
On that yolly holiday.
I go in the red
Liker a knucklehead
As I squander all
    my pay.

Oh! I yust go nuts at
    Christmas!

When the kids hang up their sock.
    It's a time for kids
        To flip their lids
            While their papa goes in hock.

I saw a nightgown for my wife
    All black and trimmed in red,
        But I don't know
            Her size and so
                She'll get a carpet sweeper
                    instead.

Oh! I yust go nuts at
    Christmas!
    On the yolly holiday
    I go in the red
    Liker a knucklehead
    As I squander all
        my pay.

Monkey Business

By Marianna K. Tu...

e were a musical family—not that the Von Trapps of *The Sound of Music* had anything to worry about in the way of competition. Each member of my family just loved to sing, but I was the shy one.

Years later as a young adult, I unearthed a small record that I had never seen before. The moment that the music began to swell, I recognized my mother's vibrant alto, my father's strong bass voice and my grandmother's sweet soprano. I have no memory of this record being made but it must have been some fun project they dreamed up in the early 1920s.

They were minus a tenor until my older brother became a teenager. So I either sat alone in our church pew on Sunday morning or sat in the choir stall next to my mother, silent, no lips moving. But I came into my own after I was married. My husband was fighting a war in Europe and I was attending an evening church service alone. At the end of the service the lady sitting in front of me turned and said, "I was wondering who had that sweet soprano voice." I recognized her as a member of a neighboring church and wished that years before I had had the courage to join my family in what they enjoyed so much—singing.

Many times when my mother rendered that selection for me, my father could hear my laughter all the way down at the barn. Only my father knew how difficult it was for my mother to allude to even a **monkey getting drunk!** *She was a true teetotaler!*

I can remember well one special song my mother used to sing to me if I was suffering from hurt feelings, disappointment or some other seeming tragedy in my young life. It never failed to hit the mark and make me forget how cruel life could be.

My youngest grandson seemed to inherit the same type of problem I had suffered. He was a frequent visitor to the beach home we

ad built for our retirement. His older brother, five years his senior, often brought a friend to spend the weekend. On these occasions, young Josh would feel like the fifth wheel, so I always made an effort to join him in the things he enjoyed most—playing miniature golf, going to the water slide or swimming in our lagoon. Oh, yes, he loved to check the crab traps, too.

But one summer afternoon I knew it was going to take more than a game of miniature golf to lift him out of the doldrums. Suddenly I could hear my mother's familiar voice lifting my spirits and making me forget that life was not so bad.

"Oh, I went to the animal fair,
All the birds and the beasts were there,
The big baboon by the light of the moon
Was combing his auburn hair.
The monkey he got drunk,
And sat on the elephant's trunk,
The elephant sneezed and fell on his knees
And that was the end of the monk."

Many times when my mother rendered that selection for me, my father could hear my laughter all the way down at the barn. Years later, when Josh stopped laughing long enough to say, "Sing it again, Nan," I clasped my hands in prayer and said, "Thank you, Mother." Only my father knew how difficult it was for my mother to allude to even a *monkey* getting drunk! She was a true teetotaler! ❖

The Animal Fair

Editor's note: We found three versions of this old children's song. The version noted by the author mentions the monkey getting drunk. Her mother would have been happy to know the other two versions do not.

Version 1
I went to the animal fair,
The birds and the beasts were there,
The big baboon, by the light of the moon,
Was combing his auburn hair,
The monkey bumped the skunk,
And sat on the elephant's trunk.
The elephant sneezed and fell to his knees,
And that was the end of the monk,
The monk, the monk, the monk.

Version 2
I went to the animal fair,
The birds and the bees were there.
The old raccoon, by the light of the moon,
Was combing his auburn hair.
The funniest was the monk,
He climbed up the elephant's trunk,
The elephant sneezed and fell to his knees,
And what became of the monk?
The monk, the monk, the monk.

Version 3
I went to the animal fair,
The birds and the beasts were there.
The big baboon, by the light of the moon,
Was combing his auburn hair.
The monkey, he got drunk,
And sat on the elephant's trunk.
The elephant sneezed and fell on his knees,
And what became of the monk?
The monk, the monk, the monk.

Roll Out the Barrel

By Helen Bolterman

I love music. And next to music, I love dancing. Putting the two together brings back memories of my teen years when I visited my grandfather's farm in Sacred Heart, Minn., during the summer. It was there that I was introduced to lively old-time bands that were favorites in the 1940s.

My favorite cousin, Jane, visited Grandfather's farm often when I was there on summer vacation. She lived with her family at a nearby farm on the outskirts of Granite Falls, Minn. Of course, I was delighted when she visited, as it could be rather boring with only adults in that household of aunts and uncles. When Jane and I were together, however, they patiently tolerated the antics of their two lively young nieces. I also often visited Jane at her home and joined her family when they visited nearby cities for shopping, outdoor movies or other activities.

Every Friday and Saturday night, the dance hall in the nearby town of Renville, Minn., buzzed with activity. When a band was hired to play for the dance there, Jane and I would use any means possible to get a ride so that we could attend. Sometimes Jane's brother, Carroll, allowed us to accompany him and his date. At his OK, we happily took our places in the open rumble seat in the rear of his vehicle. We didn't mind the wind tousling our hair as it blew around us; we were eagerly anticipating a fun evening.

Admission to the dance averaged 25–50 cents, depending on the band that had been hired. Jane and I often met some of our friends at the dance, and among them we would find willing dance partners. I was not very adept at dancing back then, but I knew some basic steps.

I believe I inherited my love of music and dancing from my father, who loved old-time dancing. On occasion, he and mother accompanied another couple to barn dances or other local dances.

It wasn't long before I was caught up in the rhythm of the music and found myself swinging with the rest of the crowd. Polka music was popular then and one song that really brought out the dancers was *The Beer Barrel Polka.* The dance hall's old pine floor rumbled and groaned under the dancing feet of young and old. True to the song's words, it would "put the blues on the run … for the gang's all here!"

As I grew older, the trips to Grandpa's farm were less frequent. But memories of those fun evenings of dance and music will remain tucked in my heart forever.

The Beer Barrel Polka continued to be a favorite of mine, and a favorite everywhere there were dancing feet. When I returned to my home in LaCrosse, Wis., I often went with my girlfriends to the Avalon Ballroom in LaCrosse where dances were held three nights a week. Friday nights featured old-time music; Saturdays were nights for the more modern dances;

> *It wasn't long before I was caught up in the rhythm of the music and found myself swinging with the rest of the crowd. Polka music was popular then and one song that really brought out the dancers was The Beer Barrel Polka.*

nd Sunday evenings were usually variety
ights. Some weekends I joined my friends for
vo or three nights of dancing. The Jerry Gilb-
rtson Band was one of our favorite groups that
layed there. Jerry could royally rock the audi-
nce with *Roll Out the Barrel* on his accordion.

When I met and later married my husband,
Wes, our favorite place to go was the Avalon
Ballroom, and there would often be requests for
The Beer Barrel Polka. I fondly remember, too,
he family picnics and family reunions where
veryone joined around the campfire for a night
f music. Sometimes someone in our group
would have a guitar and would lead us in famil-
ar songs, including *The Beer Barrel Polka*.

It was our tradition during the first years of our
marriage for Wes and I to purchase a music record
ach payday. Our collection included several ren-
itions of *The Beer Barrel Polka* by such famous
rtists of the 1940s–1950s as Guy Lombardo,

Frankie Yankovic, Jimmy Sturr, the Six Fat Dutch-
men and Myron Floren. Myron Floren, a member
of Lawrence Welk's band, which we watched on
television each Saturday night, could really tickle
the keys on his accordion, and one of his oft-
played songs was *The Beer Barrel Polka*. Years
later we had the opportunity to meet the talented
Myron Floren when we went on a bus tour. He
was the featured guest at the trip's farewell dinner
show. It was a very special evening of dancing to
our favorite music.

We hold dear those memories of the Good
Old Days, and we still love to kick up our heels.
The old Avalon Ballroom has been converted
into a restaurant, but we still continue to go to
dances at our favorite local club. And we still
dance the polka—though perhaps not so often,
and perhaps a bit slower. But even though our
feet do not kick so high, still "the blues are on
the run when we are having fun!" ❖

Roll Out the Barrel

English words by Lew Brown, 1939

There's a garden, what a garden,
Only happy faces bloom there
And there's never any room there
For a worry or a gloom there.
Oh! there's music and there's dancing
And a lot of sweet romancing
When they play the polka
They all get in the swing:

Ev'ry time they hear that oom-pa-pa,
Ev'rybody feels so tra-la-la
They want to throw their cares away,
They all go "Lah-de-ah-de-ay,"
Then they hear a rumble on the floor,

It's the big surprise they're waiting for
And all the couples form a ring
For miles around you'll hear them sing:

Chorus:
Roll out the barrel,
We'll have a barrel of fun!
Roll out the barrel,
We've got the blues on the run.
Zing! Boom! Ta-ra-rel!
Ring out a song of good cheer!
Now's the time to roll the barrel
For the gang's all here!

The Bus Ride

By Ann Oliver

*I*t is funny how a song can jog our memory of a past experience. I listen to a radio program that plays music from "the swinging years," as they call them. One day they were playing songs of the 1940s, and they played a little ditty called *Mairzy Doats* that was popular about that time. As I listened, the memories flooded back.

Those were the war years. My brother was overseas with the Army, and Dad was working in the shipyards in Houston, Texas. My mother and sisters and I lived in a little apartment in Tyler, Texas. We missed Dad and my brother, and we decided to go to Houston and visit Dad on a weekend while I was out of school. My sisters were working, so Mother and I packed a suitcase and headed down to the bus station.

We climbed aboard the Greyhound bus and started our journey at 6 o'clock in the evening. The bus would arrive in Houston at 6 in the morning—an all-night trip! With the interstate highways and fancy cars today, it is about a 4-hour drive from Tyler to Houston. As Mother said, the bus stopped at every little "pig trail" along the way. But that is how it was done back in the Good Old Days of the 1940s.

Since it was wartime, the bus was filled with soldiers and they were having a grand time singing that popular little song, *Mairzy Doats*, over and over.

If the words sound queer and funny to your ear,
    A little bit jumbled and jivey,
    Sing "mares eat oats and does eat oats
    And little lambs eat ivy."
They sang with gusto.

When we stopped on one of the many stops along the way, Mother whispered to me, "If I hear that song one more time, I will scream." We climbed back onto the bus and the soldiers had grown sleepy so the song ended as they started to doze off.

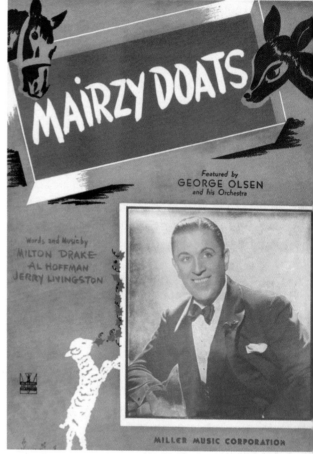

Mairzy Doats © 1943 Miller Music Corp., New York

This was my first bus ride, and I wasn't about to sleep and miss anything, so I contented myself with gazing out into the darkness. Soon the sky went from inky black to sky-blue pink and we knew we would be arriving in Houston soon.

Mother opened her purse and took out her Tangee lipstick and a small compact. She applied the lipstick to her lips, and then she put a little on a finger and rubbed it into her cheeks. She had to look pretty for her man.

The bus rolled into the big old downtown bus station and, sure enough, there was Dad, waiting for us. He took our suitcase, and we walked a short distance to the Auditorium Hotel in downtown Houston. It was a wonderful visit and I will always remember it as a special time in those war years—*Mairzy Doats* and all. ❖

Mairzy Doats

Words and music by Milton Drake, Al Hoffman and Jerry Livingston

I know a ditty nutty as a fruitcake
Goofy as a goon and silly as a loon
Some call it pretty, others call it crazy
But they all sing this tune:

Mairzy doats and dozy doats
And liddle lamzy divey
A kiddley divey too, wouldn't you?
Yes! Mairzy doats and dozy doats
And liddle lamzy divey
A kiddley divey too, wouldn't you?

If the words sound queer
And funny to your ear,
A little bit jumbled and jivey
Sing: "Mares eat oats and
      does eat oats
And little lambs eat ivy."

Oh! Mairzy doats and dozy doats
And liddle lamzy divey
A kiddley divey too, wouldn't you-oo?
A kiddley divey too, wouldn't you?

Wait for the Wagon

By R.B. Buckley and George P. Knauff

Will you come with me, my Phillis dear,
To yon blue mountain free,
Where the blossoms smell the sweetest,
Come rove along with me.
It's ev'ry Sunday morning
    when I am by your side,
We'll jump into the wagon,
    and all take a ride.

Chorus:
Wait for the wagon,
Wait for the wagon,
Wait for the wagon,
And we'll all take a ride.

Where the river runs like silver,
    and the birds they sing so sweet,
I have a cabin, Phillis,
    and something good to eat.
Come, listen to my story,
    it will relieve my heart,
So jump into the wagon,
    and off we will start.

Do you believe, my Phillis dear,

old Mike, with all his wealth,
Can make you half so happy,
    as I with youth and health?
We'll have a little farm,
    a horse, a pig, and cow,
And you will mind the dairy,
    while I will guide the plough.

Your lips are red as poppies,
    your hair so slick and neat,
All braided up with dahlias,
    and hollyhocks so sweet.
It's ev'ry Sunday morning,
    when I am by your side,
We'll jump into the wagon,
    and all take a ride.

Together, on life's journey,
    we'll travel till we stop,
And if we have no trouble,
    we'll reach the happy top.
Then come with me, sweet Phillis,
    my dear, my lovely bride,
We'll jump into the wagon,
    and all take a ride.

In My Merry Oldsmobile

Words by Vincent Bryan
Music by Gus Edwards

In My Merry Oldsmobile © 1968 by Schaum Publications, Inc. Milwaukee. Wis.

Young Johnnie Steele has an Oldsmobile.
He loves a dear little girl.
She is the queen of his gas machine.
She has his heart in a whirl.
Now when they go for a spin, you know,
She tries to learn his auto, so
He lets her steer while he gets her ear
And whispers soft and low:

Chorus:
Come away with me, Lucille,
In my merry Oldsmobile;
Down the road of life we'll fly
Automo-bubbling, you and I!
To the church we'll swiftly steal
Then our wedding bells with peal,
You can go as far as you like with me
In my merry Oldsmobile!

They love to spark in the dark old park,
As they go flying along,
She says she knows why the motor goes;
The sparker's awfully strong.
Each day they spoon to the engine's tune,
Their honeymoon will happen soon,
He'll win Lucille with his Oldsmobile
And then he'll will fondly croon:

Repeat Chorus

Five Foot Two

Words by Sam M. Lewis and Joe Young
Music by Ray Henderson

I just saw a maniac, maniac, maniac,
Wild, and tearing his hair,
Jumping like a jumpin' Jack,
Jumpin' Jack, jumpin' Jack,
Child, you should have been there,
Laughed so loud I thought that I would cave in,
When I heard that silly, daffy-dilly ravin':

Chorus:
Five foot two … eyes of blue …
But oh! What those five foot could do …
Has anybody seen my girl?
Turned-up nose … turned-down hose …
Never had no other beaus …
Has anybody seen my girl?
Now if you run into
a five foot two
Covered with fur,
Diamond rings and all those things,
Betcha' life it isn't her …
But could she love … could she woo …
Could she, could she, could she coo?
Has anybody seen my girl?

Love made him a lunatic, lunatic, lunatic,
Gee! he hollered and cried,
Like a monkey on a stick,
On a stick, on a stick,
He was fit to be tied.
When we asked him for his wife's description,
He just answered all of us with this conniption:

1930 Old Gold ad, House of White Birches nostalgia archives

Round the Mountain

By Ruth Cox Anderson

My father was the oldest of eight children. In 1926, his next-to-oldest sister, who held fifth place in the family, married a man from an even larger family. His family was pleased with the marriage and they were very sociable. "Come to visit any time," they urged us. "Any of you, all of you."

Their offers of hospitality were sincere. Besides more general invitations to "come by any time," they asked us to join them for specific events like summer picnics and Christmas Eve cookies-and-punch affairs. "As sociable as anyone in Fayette County," my father said, as if he were surprised to find a family like that living in another Ohio county (they dwelt in Ross County).

Our family—my dad, mother, sister and I—went to Grandma's right after church every Sunday and stayed until it was time to go home and milk the cows. My aunt and her husband from the big Ross County family came to Grandma's two or three Sundays a month, and almost always brought enough of her husband's clan to fill the car.

One Sunday afternoon they brought not only two of the husband's younger sisters, but two adult male cousins, carrying guitars. None of us knew these men, but Grandma and Grandpa gave them a warm welcome, as they did anyone who crossed the worn threshold to their living room. (Why there was a threshold between the dining room, through which everyone entered the house, and the living room, I don't know. But Grandpa used to say, "It's a bad year if that threshold doesn't get worn down a bit.")

Without even answering, our piano player struck up the tune, **She'll Be Coming 'Round the Mountain.**

After introductions all around, one of the guitar players said, "If it will pleasure you, we'd like to play for you. If anyone can play the piano we'll be glad to have an accompaniment." Then, realizing that there was no piano in sight and he might be causing embarrassment, he said, "If there's no piano and our entertainment is welcome, we'll just do the best we can."

Fortunately my grandparents had a piano and a daughter-in-law present who could play it. Grandma affirmed these facts, then said, "We'll just open the parlor, even if it isn't a holiday." Then she explained, "We always kept the piano in the parlor so the others wouldn't bother the one practicing."

Soon we were all gathered in the parlor. Those who couldn't find a chair brought a cushion from the living room and sat on the floor.

We sang a mixture—hymns, things like *Put On Your Old Gray Bonnet*, and classics such as *My Old Kentucky Home*. But to be truthful, all I can remember with certainty is the last song we sang.

"Everybody know this?" one of the guitar-playing cousins said. He turned to my piano-playing aunt and said, "For a closing, let's do *She'll Be Coming 'Round the Mountain*. You know that, I reckon."

Without even answering, our piano player struck up the tune. The lead guitar player turned to the rest of us as his partner strummed the first notes. "Come on," he said, "we're here to have fun! Everybody sing!"

We went through all the regular verses, singing loudly enough to shake the rafters. But there were no houses nearby, and Grandma and Grandpa owned a few hundred acres, so we could make all the noise we wanted without disturbing anyone.

As we neared the end of the last verse, the lead guitar player called out, "We're doing great, having fun! Make some verses up! Somebody call out and we'll take it up." One of Dad's brothers offered, "We'll all try to please her when she comes." The group seemed full of ideas, and we went on for a while. I remember "We won't let the boys tease her when she comes," and one I thought a little odd, "We won't let nobody seize her when she comes." That rather worried me. I wondered if somebody might seize me; of course, I wouldn't care if it was the gypsies, but were there other dangers around? By the time that verse was finished, I had decided that since I had no red pajamas—one verse had been, "She'll be wearing red pajamas when she comes"—I was probably safe.

We sang "We'll ask folks in to meet her when she comes" and "We'll fix her toast for breakfast when she comes."

Finally no one had another bright idea. Throats were getting tired, anyway, and time to milk the cows was drawing near.

My aunt closed the piano. Being cordially invited, the guitar players promised to come again. Grandma shut the parlor door before she followed us out to our cars. Never at a lack for words, Grandma thanked the guitar players for an afternoon of unexpected pleasure. She assured all of us that our company had been deeply appreciated and urged us all to visit again soon.

As we pulled away from Grandma's, Mama asked Daddy if he'd enjoyed the music. He said the hymns had been nice, and most of the other songs were all right, but he didn't think a woman had any business wearing red pajamas in public. Mama didn't answer.

My sister and I began to make up verses. The first one was "We will buy her pink pajamas when she comes." Looking back, I doubt if that was any real comfort to Daddy. I can't remember half the verses my sister and I made up. It occupied part of our free time for two or three weeks. One verse was "We'll fix her scrambled eggs for breakfast when she comes"; another was "We'll have her tell us stories when she comes." I truly believe that the path to my getting published in more than 90 periodicals began with making up verses to add to *She'll Be Coming 'Round the Mountain*.

A librarian friend of mine searched out the origin of this song and came up with the information that it was sung by slaves before the Civil War, and that the "she" referred to back then was a train. The meaning of the pronoun changed with time, and so, I suspect, did the favorite verses. ❖

She'll Be Coming 'Round the Mountain

Author Unknown

Editor's note: *The melody of this old folk song comes from an even older Negro spiritual,* When the Chariot Comes.

She'll be coming 'round the mountain
    when she comes.
She'll be coming 'round the mountain
    when she comes.
She'll be coming 'round the mountain,
She'll be coming 'round the mountain,
She'll be coming 'round the mountain
    when she comes.

She'll be driving six white horses
    when she comes. …

Oh, we'll all come out to meet her
    when she comes. …

We will kill the old red rooster
    when she comes. …

Oh, we'll all have chicken 'n' dumplin's
    when she comes. …

We'll all be shoutin' "Hallelujah"
    when she comes. …

Repeat first verse.

In Our Youth

Chapter Five

Back in the Good Old Days, many small towns had bandstands, and those structures were the centers of many important events in our youth.

The bandstand in Harrison, Ark., the small town south of our old home place, was the scene of everything from concerts to dances to political gatherings to patriotic observances. Through years of use and abuse, the old bandstand became an eyesore and finally a hazard and had to be razed.

To this day, every time I think of that old bandstand, I think of Irving Berlin's first great hit from 1911, *Alexander's Ragtime Band*. It is reminiscent of the fun we all had around and on the bandstands of our youth:

Alexander's Ragtime Band

Oh, ma honey, oh, ma honey,
Better hurry and let's meander
Ain't you goin', ain't you goin',
To the leader man,
Ragged meter man?
Oh, ma honey, oh, ma honey,
Let me take you to Alexander's
Grandstand, brass band,
Ain't you comin' along?

Oh, ma honey, oh, ma honey
There's a fiddle with notes that screeches,
Like a chicken, like a chicken
And the clarinet
Is a colored pet.
Come and listen, come and listen,
To a classical band what's peaches,
Come now, somehow,
Better hurry along.

Chorus:
Come on and hear,
Come on and hear,
Alexander's Ragtime Band,
Come on and hear,
Come on and hear,
It's the best band in the land!
They can play a bugle call
Like you never heard before,
So natural that you want to go to war
That's just the bestest band what am,
Honey Lamb!

Come on along,
Come on along,
Let me take you by the hand
Up to the man,
Up to the man,
Who's the leader of the band.
And if you want to hear
The Swanee River played in ragtime
Come on and hear,
Come on and hear,
Alexander's Ragtime Band!

About a quarter of a century ago, a new bandstand was built at the corner of the Boone County Courthouse square in downtown Harrison. I've seen weddings performed there, and recorded music has been played from it for street dances.

That's great, but I keep hoping that a community orchestra will again liven up the bandstand—maybe to the strains of *Alexander's Ragtime Band*, or any of those favorite songs we loved in our youth.

—Ken Tate

Outside of You

By Joe Curreri

Editor's note: While the author cannot remember the writers of Outside of You, *I do. The words to that wonderful old tune were penned by Al Dubin; the music was composed by Harry Warren. The song was written in 1935 for the musical Broadway Gondolier.—K.T.*

It's funny how one song, *Outside of You*, a song that no one plays or remembers anymore, could have such a powerful influence on one person.

Back during the Depression years in the 1930s, baseball was my life during the summer. In the winter it was music. We had an old player piano in our home in Philadelphia, and when I was 12, I played all the piano rolls for hours at a time, pumping and pushing the pedals. I even went further, watching the indented piano keys as the song went on, thus learning to play the song myself on the keyboard. Music filled our home in those days. We made our own entertainment with the piano and wind-up Victrola, singing and dancing. Radio came later.

Most of the songs I heard and learned at 12 were Italian since my parents had emigrated from Italy. I was happy when I played their favorite Italian folk songs and saw them smiling, singing and dancing.

> *Girls—yuk! I hated them. I never even played kissing games, like spinning the bottle, as others did. Girls—yuk!*

But in the summer, I had to get out of the stifling heat of our fanless home. I walked 3 miles to play baseball in the park now called Franklin Roosevelt Park. So, at 13 and 14, it was music, school, baseball, music and baseball. Girls were out of my mind.

Girls—yuk! I hated them. I never even played kissing games, like spinning the bottle, as others did. *Girls—yuk!*

But at 14, something happened. Puberty, followed by puppy love. The dictionary explains puberty: "The physical beginning of manhood and womanhood. Puberty comes at about 14 in boys and about 12 in girls."

In 1934, when I was 14, we played in a Fairmount Park League championship baseball game. All of our South Philly neighbors came out to root for us. When the game ended, we were champions! Exuberant neighbors piled the players into their cars for a triumphant ride home. I jumped into a Model T filled with eight people.

One neighborhood girl named Josephine, 13, with jet-black hair and sparkling eyes, sat on my lap. I thought she was cute, and I felt something strange happening to me: My hate for girls was subsiding. Josephine was something else! ❖

Puppy Love by John Slobodnik, House of White Birches nostalgia archives

In 1935 I heard a song over the radio titled *Outside of You*. It had such an impact on me that I remember the song and the words to this day. I thought it had been written especially for me. It begins:

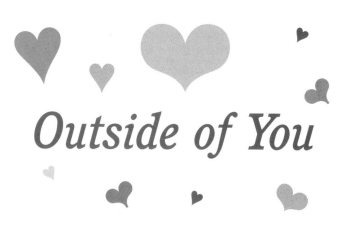

Outside of You

Words by Al Dubin
Music by Harry Warren

Gee, it's great to be absolutely free,
No one orders me around;
The girls have always found
I simply won't be bound.
Now I have a fear,
Romance may be near,
And you're the one to blame, my dear.

But it's the chorus I really enjoyed and still remember so well:

I have always been a sort of woman hater.
I have never met a girl I'd cater to.
I considered every girl an agitator
Outside of you.

That is exactly how I felt in those young years, so I learned the words and music and played it on the piano, over and over.

Look at Cleopatra and Madame DuBarry.
They were pretty bad if history is true.
I have never met the girl that I would marry
Outside of you.

I won't deny the fact that I
Thought women were a curse.
But now my hate has turned to love.
I don't know which is worse.

As you see, puppy love began to take over this young teenager.

So if you don't mind the fuss and all
  the bother,
I would like to have a wife, a kid or two,
And they should resemble no one but
  their father
Outside of you.

I never did marry my Josephine, my puppy love. We eventually walked different streets. But I did marry and had two great kids, boys, like in the song. And when they became teenagers, I played and sang the words to "my song." They understood and felt what I felt. And I did the same for my three granddaughters. And I made sure I told them that "I don't hate girls. I love them!"

I never did find out who wrote the song or the lyrics. Once in a while I still play that song—and I remember! ❖

Two Wrongs and a Right

By Audrey Corn

Music was definitely not my favorite subject back in the 1940s when I attended school in Brooklyn, N.Y. Our teacher, Miss Silvers, was strict and mean, and her songs bored me to tears.

One day, I decided to relieve the tedium by writing a note to my best friend. I tore off a sheet from my assignment pad and scribbled a brief message. Miss Silvers was playing the piano with her back to the class. The coast was clear!

I slipped the note to the kid on my left. He read the name on the outside and sent it on its way. Miss Silvers never raised her eyes from the keyboard. "Give me that note!" she bellowed.

Nobody tangled with Miss Silvers! Richard Crowley handed her the note.

"Who wrote this?" Miss Silvers demanded.

"I did," I whispered.

Miss Silvers unfolded the message and read it aloud. "I saw J looking at me. I think he likes me! We'll talk at lunch." Miss Silvers crumpled the note and threw it in the wastebasket. "Who is J?" she asked.

"John." I tried to sound brave.

"John!" Miss Silvers repeated. "All right class, we'll dedicate our next song to John." She settled herself at the piano and started to bang out the familiar chorus to *Oh Johnny, Oh, Johnny, Oh!* "Oh Johnny! Oh Johnny! How you can love! Oh Johnny! Oh Johnny! Heavens above!"

Humiliation is unbearable at any age. But in early adolescence it was devastating. I wanted to crawl under my desk and die.

Miss Silvers made us repeat the chorus twice. After that she returned to the regular lesson. Every so often, though, I caught her watching me. *The old meany.*

Suddenly Miss Silvers quit playing, right in the middle of a song. She got up from the piano and walked over to me. *Now what?* I wondered.

Miss Silvers took a deep breath. When she spoke, her voice was loud enough for everyone to hear. "I'm sorry that I embarrassed you. I should have waited and spoken to you privately after class. You were wrong to send that note, but I was equally wrong to read it out loud. Two wrongs don't make a right," she concluded.

Then she told the class to turn to page 88.

I never forgot how Miss Silvers humiliated me. But I also remember her apology—in public, in front of the whole class. Miss Silvers and her Johnny song taught me a lot more than music back in the Good Old Days. ❖

Oh Johnny, Oh Johnny, Oh!

Words by Ed Rose
Music by Abe Olman

Oh, Johnny! Oh, Johnny!
How you can love!
Oh, Johnny! Oh, Johnny!
Heavens above!
You make my sad heart jump with joy,
And when you're near I just
Can't sit still a minute.
I'm so … Oh, Johnny! Oh, Johnny!
Please tell me, do—
What makes me love you so?
You're not handsome, it's true,
But when I look at you,
I just … Oh Johnny!
Oh Johnny! Oh!

Schoolroom Music by John Slobodnik, House of White Birches nostalgia archives

Getting Our Kicks

By Robert J. Mille

A lthough we had seen much of the country through the windows of troop trains, in 1948 my brother Tom, friend Al and I decided that we'd see the U.S.A. up close and at our leisure.

During the late 1940s a popular song by Bobby Troup, *Route 66*, urged those motoring west to use the "Mother Road." The tune received a lot of exposure on our local radio stations and was featured on many jukeboxes, so we heeded the suggestion and chose that famous road for crossing the nation.

Since we lived in Philadelphia, Pa., our plan called for us to drive across the state, through Ohio and Indiana, and then up to Chicago, Ill., to access Route 66. Each of us got permission from our employers to take an extended, unpaid vacation in late July 1948.

Our vehicle was a 1947 Jeep station wagon, built by Willys-Overland in Toledo, Ohio, which I had purchased new for $1,838. It was one of the first all-metal wagons, and compared to many of today's cars, it was big, seating six adults. By 1947 standards, however, it was rather small. Nonetheless, it was a real station wagon— the seats were removable and a huge tailgate opened down flat with the floor to convert the car into a sturdy cargo hauler.

In an era of sixes and eights, it was underpowered with a tiny, 4-cylinder engine of 63 horsepower taken from the Jeep of World War II. There was no air conditioning or power steering, no power brakes, electric windows or radio. There wasn't even an oil filter! Before taking to the road, my brother and I added an oil filter, gasoline filter heater, radio, windshield washer, turn signals, spare-tire cover, fog lights and carpeting.

Our trip lasted almost four weeks and took us through 19 states. We dis-

Our friend Al prepared meals on a Sterno stove perched on the wagon's lowered tailgate.

dained motels; instead, we removed the rear seats at night and camped by the roadside, bedding down on the wagon's flat floor. There was little fear of being bothered by passersby; ours was a less violent society in those days. Indeed, as we proceeded westward, the people

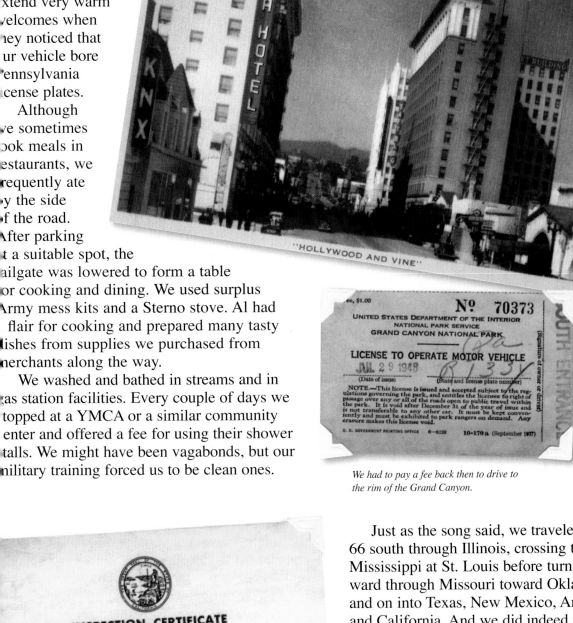

...ve met seemed to extend very warm welcomes when they noticed that ...ur vehicle bore ...ennsylvania ...icense plates.

Although ...ve sometimes ...ook meals in ...estaurants, we ...requently ate ...y the side ...f the road. ...fter parking ...t a suitable spot, the ...ailgate was lowered to form a table ...or cooking and dining. We used surplus ...rmy mess kits and a Sterno stove. Al had ... flair for cooking and prepared many tasty ...ishes from supplies we purchased from ...erchants along the way.

We washed and bathed in streams and in ...as station facilities. Every couple of days we ...topped at a YMCA or a similar community ...enter and offered a fee for using their shower ...talls. We might have been vagabonds, but our ...ilitary training forced us to be clean ones.

We had to pay a fee back then to drive to the rim of the Grand Canyon.

...vehicles entering California were inspected for "contraband" fruits and ...bles. We had to surrender three Sunkist oranges purchased in New Mexico, ...with half a loaf of bread and a few potatoes.

Just as the song said, we traveled Route 66 south through Illinois, crossing the great Mississippi at St. Louis before turning westward through Missouri toward Oklahoma and on into Texas, New Mexico, Arizona and California. And we did indeed pass through the towns made famous by the song—Kingman, Barstow, San Bernardino.

In the Los Angeles area we checked into a motel in Pasadena and spent a few days seeing the sights. Like all tourists, we signed on for a couple of guided tours to see Hollywood and all it had to offer.

We decided to expand our trip on the way home by selecting a route that took us through central California, Nevada, Utah, Colorado, Kansas, Nebraska and Iowa. After leaving Illinois, we detoured into Michigan

Al (left) and Tom in the Mojave Desert. At sunrise we found the morning air quite cool.

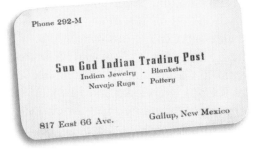

to visit a friend who lived in Battle Creek. One memorable event occurred when we encountered a summer snowstorm while cresting the Rockies outside Denver, Colo.

Nearing home, we stopped to visit some relatives who lived in a small town nestled in the mountains of northwestern Pennsylvania. There we picked up a passenger, a cousin who asked for a ride to Atlantic City, N.J., in order to spend a couple of weeks with a sister who lived there. Our coast-to-coast jaunt was completed when we strolled the beaches of that resort city.

All told, our trip was rather inexpensive. We started with a pool of $300 for car expenses. We returned with $16.22. We used 379 gallons of gas, which cost $138.96 for a distance of 7,423 miles. Repairs consisted of a new tire, a front wheel alignment, a new fan belt, a tune-up and a couple of oil changes and lube jobs.

The Willys performed admirably in all kinds of weather—high humidity on the East Coast, severe thunderstorms on the Great Plains, oppressive heat in the Mojave Desert, abrasive winds on Great Salt Lake and low atmospheric pressure in the Rockies. Our trip showed that the Jeep's "ugly" shape had an advantage over the sleek, streamlined beauties of the day. It had natural air conditioning long before the installation of mechanical air coolers in cars. After passing a number of stalled cars whose engines had overheated in the summer heat, I concluded that the Jeep's squared-off front end with its built-in air scoops and splash pans was very efficient in directing cooling air through the engine compartment to keep under-hood temperatures at proper levels. And after noticing that passengers in passing stylish cars seemed to be perspiring, I appreciated the fact that by opening the Jeep's front cowl scoop and upper rear door, a refreshing draft quickly dissipated any stifling heat in the passenger compartment. What a wonderful feature on hot days!

The vehicle's reliability and utility enabled us to realize our boyhood dreams of seeing places like the fabled Mississippi River, the storied Texas Panhandle, the amazing Petrified Forest, the awesome Grand Canyon, the forbidding

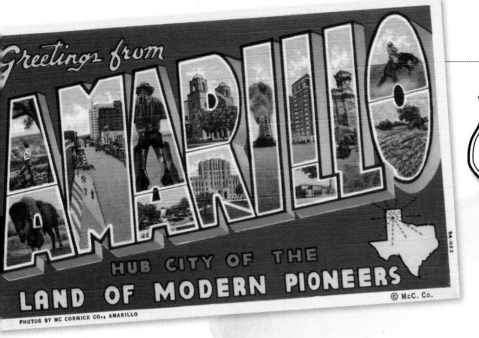

Mojave Desert, the historic Old West, glamorous Hollywood and the great Pacific Ocean. We enjoyed every moment of that journey across the country!

Even today, whenever *Route 66* is played on some nostalgia radio program, it brings back fond memories of that once-in-a-lifetime trip of so long ago. It reminds me of that first new car and how well it served us. The song may have faded into obscurity, but just thinking about it evokes pleasant memories of those youthful, carefree times in the Good Old Days!❖

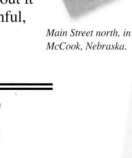

Main Street north, in McCook, Nebraska.

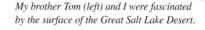

My brother Tom (left) and I were fascinated by the surface of the Great Salt Lake Desert.

Route 66

by Bobby Troup

If you ever plan to motor west,
travel my way; take the highway that's the best.
Get your kicks on Route 66!

Well, it winds from Chicago to L.A.,
More than 2,000 miles all the way.
Get your kicks on Route 66!

Well, you go through St. Louis, Joplin, Missouri,
and Oklahoma City is mighty pretty;
You see Amarillo, Gallup, New Mexico,

Flagstaff, Arizona; don't forget Winona,
Kingman, Barstow, San Bernardino.

Won't you get hip to this timely tip
when you make that California trip,
Get your kicks on Route 66!

Heart Tugger

By Bob Pettes

When I was 10 years old, my mother suggested it might be fun for me to attend vacation Bible school at a nearby Baptist church. I was not of the same persuasion, but I consented to give it a try. I made the obligatory craft article as a gift for Mom, but the "graduation" ceremony changed my life.

We had memorized and rehearsed this hymn over and over, but when we stood before our parents and sang the entire song before the audience, tears rolled down my cheeks and lumps crowded my throat.

This song made a true believer out of me, and it has followed me through all my life.

God, Who Touches Earth With Beauty

God, who touches earth with beauty
Make me lovely, too.
Keep me ever by Thy spirit
Firm and strong and true.

Like the streams of running water
Make me crystal pure.
Like the rocks of towering grandeur
Make me strong and sure.

Like the arching of the heavens
Lift my thoughts above.
Turn my dreams to noble actions,
Ministries of love.

God, who touches earth with beauty
Make me grand and free.
Like the straightness of the pine tree,
Let me upright be.

I have remembered this for nearly 70 years now. Perhaps all the words aren't quite correct because I've never seen this song in print, but this is how I recall the verses. I still sing it to myself, and it still evokes lumps in my throat. ❖

© *Strawberry Sunday* by Bob Pettes

1894

Highland Park
JUNE 13
ICE CREAM
SOCIAL
SPONSORED BY
LADIES AID

© BOB PETTES

Johnny's Song

By Kate Hartnell Stobbe

Webster defines "song" as a relatively short metrical composition for, or suitable for singing as, a ballad or simple lyric.

In retrospect, it seems that my family could be considered "sorta" musical. Mother played the piano quite well, as did Grandma—mostly Christmas carols. Dad was always singing, vaguely imitating Caruso. Uncle played recognizable songs on an accordion. Aunt Bee was a real buzz on her mandolin.

If not playing their respective instruments, the Victrola was spinning records and everyone in the family was singing along. (I wonder what Grandma's neighbors thought, since most of this activity took place at her home?)

But most of my story revolves around Aunt Bee, Mother's sister. She was a multitalented lady who taught school in St. Louis County (fourth-graders); a special arts teacher; a Girl Scout leader; and she traveled extensively during the summer months to further her teaching career.

As a Scout leader, she learned many songs to teach her young charges. By age 3, in the 1920s, I was singing many of the ditties that Auntie had patiently taught me. One song became my all-time favorite. It was titled *Johnny Ver Beck.*

I'm not sure how recognizable the words were at that age.

One beautiful spring morning, Auntie took me to her school—I suppose as an introduction to what the future held for me. She asked me to sing the song before we left home just to be sure the words came out right. And she said, "When I tilt my head to the right and smile, I would like you to walk to the front of the classroom and sing your song. My students are expecting you and want to hear you sing *Johnny Ver Beck.*"

I was too young to have stage fright, so the song went well, and I heard my first round of applause.

After this encouraging beginning, Aunt Bee began using "head tilt and smile" as a cue for me to perform often, mostly for family and her teacher friends. I quickly learned to love the praise and approval that everyone was kind enough to shower on me.

A few weeks later, as was our weekly custom, our family attended church en masse. Organ music, prayers and singing preceded the start of our Sunday service. Just as our minister, Dr. James, approached the pulpit, I looked at Aunt Bee. She was smiling and tilting her head. I immediately rose from the pew and arrived at the pulpit a second before Dr. James.

At the finish of *Johnny Ver Beck*, a surprised church full of worshipers looked at me askance … until our minister began clapping and patted my head.

As we left the church, I heard my aunt tell Mother, "I was only leaning over and smiling at my teacher friend, Mary Barnhardt, the next pew over." ❖

Johnny Ver Beck

There was a little Dutchman,
His name was Johnny Ver Beck.
He was a dealer in sausages
And sauerkraut and speck.
He made the finest sausages that ever
    had been seen
Until one day he invented a wonderful machine

Chorus:
Oh, Mr. Johnny Ver Beck,
How could you be so mean?
We told you you'd be sorry for
Inventing that machine.
All the neighbors' cats and dogs
Will never more be seen,
They'll all be ground to sausages
In Johnny Ver Beck's machine.

Good Night, Sweetheart

By Ginger K. Nelson

"Good night, sweetheart, till we meet tomorrow," my mother sang to me each night when I was a child. Although the lyrics sound like a love song to someone's special beau, it was my mother's way of telling me that she would always love me, that I was my parents' sweetheart and always would be, and she wanted it to be the last thought I heard from her lips before I drifted off to sleep.

It became our special "tuck-in song," one that was part of our nighttime ritual for several years. I can still hear her voice, a little rough around the edges although always in tune, crooning to me, her only child, who wanted songs more often than stories.

Mom and Dad had waited several years before they knew I'd be coming. They savored the moments spent wallpapering the nursery, buying the crib and attending the baby showers, which enabled friends to give gifts of welcome.

When I was born, I was their little rosebud whose tiny mouth was often shaped like an "o." My family delighted in the fact that the hospital nurses were so enamored of me. Grandma, Grandpa, aunts, uncles and cousins, all of them somewhat prejudiced, thought I was the most beautiful baby they'd ever seen.

At that time, Daddy worked in New York City and Mom was a full-time mother in a New Jersey suburb. She delighted in the moments when she would dance around the room with me in her arms, crooning favorite tunes like *Good Night, Sweetheart.*

Both Mom and Daddy are gone now. Daddy left this earth in 1954 and Mom in 2001. There were many years when my mom and her sister, who now lived with us, moved whenever our family did, following us across the country during our Air Force stint. There were many years when both Mom and Butchie took trips with their new friends in California, Maryland and Alabama. There were many years when neither one could travel except vicariously, when we did. Finally we all stopped traveling and attended to health issues.

When my mother died, I found souvenirs— treasures of her enjoyment from time spent with her daughter—a baby-shower invitation, a baby book inscribed with all of my first accomplishments, a box of photographs from my special baby moments. There I was, sitting on the grass with a pout that would have made a movie star proud. There I was, in the crocheted peach outfit my mother made me, looking up at her as if she held the keys to all the sunshine in the world. And there I was, playing in my sandbox, grinning as if I'd just won the lottery. I cried over the photos, then set them aside for later smiles.

To my parents, I was their little sweetheart. And although I'm sure most parents feel the same way about their children, I believe I'm special when I think of that song that my mother sang to me those 64 years ago. I still hear her voice singing to me through the years. I still feel her mother's love wrapped around me all the time, but especially when I hear *Good Night, Sweetheart.* And when I get to heaven, I expect her to greet me with that song. ❖

Good Night, Sweetheart

Words and music by Ray Noble,
Jimmy Campbell and Reg Connelly

Good night, sweetheart,
Till we meet tomorrow,
Good night, sweetheart,
Sleep will banish sorrow.
Tears and parting
May make us forlorn,
But with the dawn
A new day is born,
So I'll say …

Good night, sweetheart,
Tho' I'm not beside you,
Good night, sweetheart,
Still my love will guide you.
Dreams enfold you,
In each one I'll hold you.
Good night, sweetheart,
Good night.

Christmas in Any Language

By Doris Breck

Mother loved music. She would have had to, to put up with the old reed organ, which had just about wheezed its last notes. She sometimes attempted to play a few simple songs on it by ear; we small kids didn't have much to do with it other than twirling on the round stool.

She had been hinting about getting a piano for some time. Dad, on the other hand, thought a phonograph would give a lot of music and be a nice piece of furniture; and besides, it would give us kids some exercise winding it up! He suggested a battery radio, too—one like the neighbors had that brought in music and the weather, even market reports. But Mother was adamant. "The children should be given a chance to learn to play an instrument."

Later, as we trooped into our local music store, it was understood that we were in the market for a good used piano. New ones were expensive, and although the potato crop had been good and Dad had hauled three or four loads to the warehouse for shipping, I knew he hoped to purchase a manure spreader so he wouldn't have to load the wagon with a fork.

Whatever the case, an enthusiastic salesman said he'd show us what they had in stock, but just for fun he wanted us to hear a roll on a brand-new player piano. I don't know when Dad decided that the beautiful mahogany upright was more important than the convenient spreader, but when the merchant followed up the zealous salesman with an offer of a free roll that he had played—*Stille Nacht (Silent Night)*—Dad's last shreds of resistance evaporated.

We got our piano just in time for Christmas. A long, polished bench replaced the worn organ stool, and inside the bench there was room for a dozen or more rolls. In time, our collection would overflow to the bottom shelf of the library table, but since rolls were a dollar or more, they were bought sparingly.

The piano was joyfully crowded into the parlor with a large leather davenport and rocker, the table and a fernery, with a corner reserved for the usual big white pine tree. With Christmas so close, we were permitted to go into the parlor each evening, French doors open for warmth, to give Mother a chance to hear her favorite holiday song, which we "pedaled out" while she finished the day's household tasks. Usually, wiping her hands on her apron, she would join us in singing the last verse.

The words were printed in both the languages she knew—German and English—on one side of the roll. I couldn't read the words Mother sang. She said they were in the language that our father and she had known during their childhood in the old country. I asked her if they had celebrated Christmas there, too, and she assured me that the birth of the Christ child is observed in almost every land. Her eyes seemed to be misty during the song. After that, I didn't think the words looked funny any more. They were telling us about Silent Night, too, only in a different way.

Mother hoped that one of us would want to learn to play the piano. Eventually I was the one who took the opportunity. My sister was more interested in reading books and my brother preferred roaming the woods and pastures.

Mother signed me up with Miss Farwell for a $1.50 weekly lesson, paid for by the faithful flock of laying hens. I enjoyed a certain amount of prestige, and the first few lessons were rather pleasant. However, the intimidating sharps and flats soon loomed threateningly on the page, and more and more my fingers were patted to remind them to stay in the right place! It was with a sigh of relief that the summer ended. (Due to uncertain road conditions and the chilliness of the parlor in winter, it had been decided I was to take lessons only in the summer months.)

I endured another summer with little progress, and after that, Mother seemed resigned to the fact that, as Dad said, "Everybody can't play. Some have to be listeners." So I was free to slide back to picking out a few tunes like *Mother, Mother, May I Go?* I was free, too, to pedal the roll *Stille Nacht* as often as my mother wanted to hear it—usually every day after the first snowfall.

The years and we children—and eventually grandchildren—took their toll. The paper on the rolls became brittle and the fastening hooks tore off. And even as our supply of usable rolls dwindled, the air pump began to fail. Though repairs would have been possible and a few rolls continued to be manufactured, it seemed like a needless expense since radio and television had taken over. The upright became little more than a roomy stand for family pictures, its old capacity all but forgotten. But even now, at holiday time, I'll hear a rendition of *Silent Night* on the radio, and all the memories come flooding back.

Most of all, I remember what my mother had said—that the Christmas story of the Christ child's birth and the wonder of it all can be told in many different languages. ❖

Silent Night, Holy Night

Words by Joseph Mohr
Music by Franz Gruber

Silent night! Holy night!
All is calm, all is bright;
Round yon virgin mother and child,
Holy infant so tender and mild,
Sleep in heavenly peace,
Sleep in heavenly peace.

Silent night! Holy night!
Shepherds quake at the sight;
Glories stream from heaven afar,
Heav'nly hosts sing "Alleluia,
Christ the Savior is born!
Christ the Savior is born!"

Silent night! Holy night!
Son of God,
Love's pure light;
Radiant beams from Thy holy face
With the dawn of redeeming grace,
Jesus, Lord, at Thy birth,
Jesus, Lord, at Thy birth.

Home & the Old Folks

Chapter Six

Janice and I were blessed with three children. Our oldest was a boy, followed by two girls. Like a lot of fathers back in the Good Old Days, I was the bread-winner, the chief disciplinarian and the familial head of state. But it was Janice who kept the familial *ship* of state steady and on course. I might have been the fuel and the engine driving the ship, but she was the rudder and the compass.

Piano lessons for our daughter Robin is a perfect example.

I played banjo and guitar. I had uncles who played guitar, mandolin and fiddle. These were instruments I could relate to. Easy to carry, easy to tune, and we had plenty of teachers ready and willing to take the skills to the next generation.

But piano? I knew nothing about playing a piano. We didn't have a piano. Piano lessons were miles away from our country home. My inclination was to be practical, but Robin's heart was set on playing piano, and Janice's heart was set on taking care of Robin's impracticality.

So, first we found a way to get Robin to lessons. Then, a few years down the road, we found a piano for the house. The family recitals, the church recitals, the sheer joy of hearing melodies wafting from the living room—all were made possible by my forward-thinking compass. Today Robin is a fairly accomplished pianist.

Thinking back to those days, I am reminded of one of my favorite songs of home and hearth. It may be true that a man's home is his castle, but "the hand that rocks the cradle … rules the world."

—*Ken Tate*

The Hand That Rules the World
Words and music by Don Fielding

They say that man is mighty,
He governs land and sea,
He wields a mighty sceptre
O'er lesser pow'rs that be.
But mightier pow'r and stronger
Man from his throne has hurled,
For the hand that rocks the cradle
Is the hand that rules the world.

In deep mysterious conclave,
'Mid philosophic minds,
Unrav'ling knotty problems,
His native sphere man finds.
Yet all his "ics" and "isms"
To heav'n's four winds are hurled,
But the hand that rocks the cradle
Is the hand that rules the world.

Behold the brave commander
Staunch 'mid the carnage stand,
Behold the guidon dying
With the colors in his hand;
Brave men they be, yet craven,
When this banner is unfurled,
For the hand that rocks the cradle
Is the hand that rules the world.

Great statesmen govern nations;
Kings mould a people's fate;
But the unseen hands of velvet
These giants regulate.
The iron hand of fortune
With woman's hand is purled
But the hand that rocks the cradle
Is the hand that rules the world.

Piano Lesson by Paula Vaughan © Copyright Newmark USA 200

Home's Not Merely Four Square Walls

By Charles Swain

Home's not merely four square walls,
Though with pictures hung and gilded;
Home is where affection calls,
Filled with shrines the heart hath builded.
Home! go, watch the faithful dove,
Sailing 'neath the heaven above us;
Home is where there's one to love,
Home is where there's one to love us.
Home is where there's one to love,
Home is where there's one to love us.

Home's not merely roof and room,
Needs it something to endear it;
Home is where the heart can bloom;
Where there's some kind lip to cheer it.
What is home with none to meet,
None to welcome, none to greet us?
Home is sweet and only sweet
Where there's one we love to meet us.
Home is sweet and only sweet
Where there's one we love to meet us.

Welcome Home by Don Sherwood, House of White Birches nostalgia archive

God Will Take Care of You

By Grace Case

Early in my marriage I learned to trust in a Higher Power. Because of it, I believe many near-tragedies were averted. I found it such a wonderful promise: "Be not dismayed, whate'er betide; God will take care of you."

My six journeys to bring our children here were all safe journeys. The hymn, my prayer, went with me. "Beneath His wings of love abide."

When my husband worked with a tractor on a steep hillside, he drove too close to the edge. The grade was almost straight up and down. The tractor skidded sideways on the frosty grass, all the way down the bank, while he thought it might overturn at any moment. "Through days of toil, where heart doth fail, God will take care of you."

When Joe, our oldest son, was 15, his left hand was severely injured while he was using a combine on a neighbor's farm. His hand was caught between the rollers on the combine and was badly burned, mashed and torn when he pulled it out. He drove the tractor home, and I rushed him to the hospital.

"Please, God, don't let a tire go flat now," I whispered while Joe huddled in the backseat, numb with shock and pain. The wound was filled with dirt and grease, making it difficult to clean.

The first two weeks weren't quite so bad. But after his hand healed, there came three more weeks of lying in the hospital.

"Oh, Mom. It hurts so awful." Joe's face screwed up in suffering. Sweat stood out on his forehead most of the time and his face was drawn and pale.

I hated not being with him every minute, and yet, seeing the agony on his face was hard to take.

"If only I could be any way but on my back," Joe moaned. He looked out the window. "If only I could just go outside … go home."

Like all mothers, I wished I could take his suffering on myself. Mothers are more used to pain. Then one afternoon, when the pain was extra severe, I told him, "While I'm gone home to get supper, Joe, pray! Then maybe when Dad and I come after supper, then maybe … maybe the pain won't be so bad."

I couldn't remember *telling* him to say his prayers since he had been a little boy. As I looked back over my shoulder before I left, he added, "And say, Mom, you pray, too."

When my husband and I went back after supper, Joe's face held a look of quiet peace, free from suffering, like an inner light was shining. His eyes no longer looked like those of a trapped animal.

Prayer—Joe's and mine—had changed things.

It's a good thing a mother has prayer to rely upon. How else could we hold home and hearth together back in the Good Old Days? ❖

God Will Take Care of You

Words by C.D. Martin
Music by W.S. Martin

Be not dismayed whate'er betide,
God will take care of you;
Beneath His wings of love abide,
God will take care of you.

Chorus:
God will take care of you,
Through' ev'ry day, O'er all the way;
He will take care of you,
God will take care of you.

Through days of toil when heart doth fail,
God will take care of you;

When dangers fierce your path assail,
God will take care of you.

All you may need He will provide,
God will take care of you;
Nothing you ask will be denied,
God will take care of you.

No matter what may be the test,
God will take care of you;
Lean, weary one, upon His breast,
God will take care of you.

Silver Threads and the Broken Heart

By Janet Hampton

"*S*ilver threads among the gold, it is hard to die alone ..."
These were the last words written in a Philadelphia rooming house by Hart Pease Danks, composer of the immortal ballad, *Silver Threads Among the Gold*. Before he could finish the sentence, he passed into a sleep that knows no awakening.

These were the last words written in a Philadelphia rooming house by Hart Pease Danks, composer of the immortal ballad, **Silver Threads Among the Gold.** *Before he could finish the sentence, he passed into a sleep that knows no awakening.*

Back in 1872, we find Hart Pease Danks alternately spending his time as a singer in a quartet and composing sacred songs. These were the golden days, when songwriting and music publishing were not the standard pursuits they are today.

Danks had casually come across a poem used as a space filler in a Wisconsin farm magazine. It had been written by the magazine's editor, Eben E. Rexford. Sensing the possibilities of writing music for this poem, he purchased it from the author for $3.

So gratified was Editor Rexford with his unexpected source of income that he immediately forwarded a batch of new poems to Danks and offered them to the composer for the same price of $3 each. Included among them was *Silver Threads Among the Gold*.

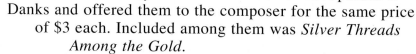

In these lyrics, Danks, a sentimentalist and much in love with his wife, caught something that was precious to him. It was the comforting thought that although "life was fading fast away," there would always remain the great consolation, an undying love for his own wife.

So the bard struck a melody that was something more than a mere tune. It included a haunting wistfulness, perhaps a dissipation of the fear of old age between two faithful lovers and a sincere affirmation of fidelity even if death was right around the corner.

Upon completing the music, Danks sold it to a publisher in Philadelphia who forwarded a copy to Chicago. It was to be sung by minstrels, then in vogue. This was practically the only method available for popularizing ballads during that era.

The tune became an instant success. But by some unaccountable irony of fate, the composer became estranged from his wife in 1873, and they remained apart until his death in 1903. *Silver Threads Among the Gold* kept selling throughout the country until it passed the 2 million mark.

When Richard Jose, the famous tenor, included this ballad in his program during the 1907 season, it could not but affect listeners as it had the previous generation. It certainly is no accident that the ballad has lived more than 100 years past its era and is still hummed, whistled and sung by people today—a true indication of an immortal song.

However, when the landlady of a certain rooming house in Philadelphia in 1903 discovered Danks' body with the unfinished message scrawled on a copy of his unforgettable song, one knew that here was a tragedy more poignant than was ever enacted upon the stage. ❖

Silver Threads Among the Gold

Words by Eben E. Rexford
Music by Hart Pease Danks

Darling, I am growing, growing old;
Silver threads among the gold
Shine upon my brow today;
Life is fading fast away.
But, my darling, you will be, will be
Always young and fair to me.
Yes, my darling, you will be
Always young and fair to me.

Chorus:
Darling, I am growing, growing old;
Silver threads among the gold
Shine upon my brow today;
Life is fading fast away.

When your hair is silver white
And your cheeks no longer bright
With the roses of the May,
I will kiss your lips and say,
"Oh, my darling, mine alone, alone,
You have never older grown.

"Yes, my darling, mine alone
"You have never older grown."

Love can never more grow old;
Locks may lose their brown and gold;
Cheeks may fade and hollow grow;
But the hearts that love will know
Never, never winter's frost and chill;
Summer's warmth is in them still;
Never, winter's frost and chill;
Summer's warmth is in them still.

Love is always young and fair;
What to us is silver hair,
Faded cheeks or steps grown slow,
To the hearts that beat below?
Since I kissed you, mine alone, alone,
You have never older grown.
Since I kissed you, mine alone, alone,
You have never older grown.

Seeing Nellie Home

In the sky the bright stars glittered,
On the bank the pale moon shone;
And 'twas from Aunt Dinah's quilting party,
I was seeing Nellie home.

Chorus:
I was seeing Nellie home,
I was seeing Nellie home;
And 'twas from Aunt Dinah's quilting party,
I was seeing Nellie home.

On my arm a soft hand rested,
Rested light as ocean foam;

And 'twas from Aunt Dinah's quilting party,
I was seeing Nellie home.

On my lips a whisper trembled,
Trembled till it dared to come;
And 'twas from Aunt Dinah's quilting party,
I was seeing Nellie home.

On my life new hopes were dawning,
And those hopes have liv'd and grown;
And 'twas from Aunt Dinah's quilting party,
I was seeing Nellie home.

Quilting Bee by Charles Berger, House of White Birches nostalgia archive

Silver-Haired Daddy of Mine

In a vine-covered shack in the mountain,
Bravely fighting the battle of time
Is a dear one who's weathered life's sorrows,
'Tis that silver-haired Daddy of mine.
If I could recall all the heartaches,
Dear old Daddy, I've caused you to bear,
If I could erase those lines on your face
And bring back the gold to your hair,

If God would but grant me the power,
Just to turn back the pages of time,
I'd give all I own if I could but atone,
To that silver-haired Daddy of mine.
I know it's too late, dear old Daddy,
To repay for the sorrow and care
But dear Mother is waiting in Heaven
Just to comfort and solace you there.

Cooling Off With Lemonade by John Slobodnik, House of White Birches nostalgia archives

My Nostalgic Song

By Margie D. Yablonski

song can take you back in time and make it stand still for one brief moment. Nostalgia can be very seductive. The song *Cielito Lindo* has that affect on me to this very day.

In the early 1930s, Mother had an old player piano that had been given to her many years before. Only two rolls of music came with it, and although they were lovely tunes, the songs were not familiar to any of us. But Mother didn't mind. She just kept pumping away every chance she had. We children, however, got tired of hearing those two tunes over and over again.

We complained so much that my father got an idea. Since my mother's birthday was a week away, he decided to buy her a new piano roll. He had it wrapped and presented it to her with a big birthday kiss. Mother was so ecstatic that she couldn't wait to play it. The song was *Cielito Lindo*.

Mother was familiar with the melody and asked my father why he had picked this particular song. "Because it's a Spanish song," he said, "and you have beautiful Spanish eyes." It seemed she never stopped playing it.

> *Although we are French-Italian, we loved and enjoyed all kinds of music, for music has always been an integral part of our family; it did not matter what its ethnic origin was.*

It then became my father's routine to pick up a new piano roll for her every day. Eventually he had to keep a list of what songs he bought so as to avoid duplications. As time went on, Mother accumulated many new and old songs.

Although we are French-Italian, we loved and enjoyed all kinds of music, for music has always been an integral part of our family; it did not matter what its ethnic origin was. But *Cielito Lindo* became Mother's all-time favorite. (After all, didn't she have Spanish eyes?)

Every time we had a party, Mother would sit at that piano, and she never moved from it. She always started with *Cielito Lindo*, then went on to many other songs while we'd all sing along. And it never failed; she always ended with her favorite song again.

During the 1950s, I was taking zither lessons. After I had learned something about music theory and how to read music and had practiced scales until I wanted to scream, my teacher felt I was ready to read sheet music and asked me what song I wanted

host. I told him *Cielito Lindo*. He warned me
that it was a difficult piece, as it had a Latin beat.
But with that song sheet before me, it was like
magic. The melody flowed effortlessly beneath
my fingers. This was *never* the case when I
played any other new piece for the first time.

By this time my father was gone and Mother
lived alone. I spent every Sunday with her. I
would bring my zither and music to practice
whatever new piece I was working on. Whenever I started to practice, Mother would always
ask, "Honey, when are you going to play my
favorite song?"

We would both break out in laughter and say
in unison, "*Cielito Lindo*."

I have several cassettes featuring this song,
and I play them at home and in my car. It takes
me back to those days so long ago when I was
just a child, and Mother would play the song
over and over again. Times change but memories are forever. Life is like a mirror and will
reflect back to the thinker what has become
indelible in the mind.

Mother is gone now, and though I do not
play my zither too often anymore, every April
8, my mother's birthday, I take it out, tune it up
and play *Cielito Lindo*. Then I look upward and
whisper, "This is for you, Mom." ❖

Cielito Lindo

By Quirino Mendoza y Cortes and Fernandez

De la sierra morena
Viene bajando viene bajando
Un par de ojitos negros
Cielito lindo de contrabando

Ese lunar que tienes
Cielito lindo junto a la boca
No se lo des a nadie
Cielito lindo que a mí me toca

Ay ay ay ay
Canta y no llores
Porque cantando se alegran
Cielito lindo los corazones

t Cozy Evening by Ron Delli Colli, House of White Birches nostalgia archives

Blest Be the Tie That Binds

By Dale Geise

*T*eenage years were a time when we all needed somebody older, a good and kind adult, to guide us. That example helped us find our way, choosing from so many paths toward the life to come.

Outside my own home, I had a whole family of examples. Albert and Gertrude Peterson, their daughter, Beverly, and sons, Jimmy and Danny, provided a second home for me when I worked for them on a hilltop farm near the little hamlet of Underwood in southwest Iowa.

After plowing the steep hillsides that Albert called Mount Baldy and Mount Beastly, I sat at the enameled table in their kitchen surrounded by talk of how much I meant to them and the give-and-take of a loving family. Gertrude filled my plate with the wondrous roast beef and mashed potatoes and gravy that still make me hunch my shoulders and smile 55 years later.

She wrote family letters to me when I was in Korea, telling of Beverly's boyfriend getting stuck in the mud on their hill after a Li'l Abner-Daisy Mae school dance. With much discussion and with much reluctance, mother and daughter woke Albert, who started the John Deere and pulled Li'l Abner out.

She wrote of Jim and Dan opening Fort Bridger, a play fort near the creek. Then they roamed the woods looking for Black Bart, the bad bandit. Those stories from home sustained me on bitterly cold Korean nights and bound my heart ever tighter to the little family "on the hill."

Gertrude was vigorous in all things, helping to pick corn by hand and not tolerating a balky team. She drove the horses home one day without the wagon. They had been struggling with a modest load of corn, pretending a small ditch was too much for them. Gertrude gave a disgusted yank back on the reins and they obediently shuffled swiftly backward, letting the wagon bang back into the ditch and breaking the "reach." There was no blaming or argument. Albert calmly helped unload the corn into another wagon and fixed the break.

I often stayed awhile in the evening until the children went to bed. Albert always went to the bedroom door, leaned in and said, "I love you." That example and so many others they set for me will last forever.

My fond memory in that church is of Albert, sitting on the right side and about halfway back, singing in his booming baritone the grand hymn **Blest Be the Tie That Binds.**

Our little clapboard church, long since gone, sat on the main street of Underwood. We entered through an 8-foot by 8-foot vestibule; the knotted rope hanging from its ceiling provided an honor for kids who were selected to ring the bell. My cousins, Wayne and Gene, and my brother, Dudley, and I sat in the back row when our confirmation times approached and took sermon notes. I still have some that are fairly serious.

My fond memory in that church is of Albert, sitting on the right side and about halfway back, singing in his booming baritone the grand hymn *Blest Be the Tie That Binds*. Any whispering stopped in the back row as Albert's voice ranged far above all others. I hushed and listened. My feelings for Albert and Gertrude and their family were gathered in that hymn: "… our hearts in Christian love … and often for each other flows the sympathizing tear."

Now I wait with anticipation and memories when the old hymn is posted for our worship services in Ames, Iowa. The love and togetherness we seek for all humanity, the same love and togetherness that came to me from a dear family of my youthful days, is summed up in *Blest Be the Tie That Binds*. ❖

Blest Be the Tie That Binds

Words by John Fawcett
Music by Hans G. Nageli

Blest be the tie that binds
Our hearts in Christian love;
The fellowship of kindred minds
Is like to that above.

Before our Father's throne,
We pour our ardent prayers;
Our fears, our hopes our aims are one,
Our comforts and our cares.

We share our mutual woes,
Our mutual burdens bear;
And often for each other flows
The sympathizing tear.

When we asunder part,
It gives us inward pain;
But we shall still be joined in heart,
And hope to meet again.

This glorious hope revives
Our courage by the way,
While each in expectation lives
And longs to see the day.

From sorrow, toil, and pain,
And sin we shall be free
And perfect love and friendship reign
Through all eternity.

What a Friend We Have in Jesus

What a friend we have in Jesus,
    All our sins and griefs to bear!
What a privilege to carry
    Everything to God in prayer!
O what peace we often forfeit,
    O what needless pain we bear,
All because we do not carry
    Everything to God in prayer.

Have we trials and temptations?
    Is there trouble anywhere?
We should never be discouraged;
    Take it to the Lord in prayer.
Can we find a friend so faithful
    Who will all our sorrows share?
Jesus knows our every weakness;
    Take it to the Lord in prayer.

Are we weak and heavy laden,
    Cumbered with a load of care?
Precious Savior, still our refuge,
    Take it to the Lord in prayer.
Do your friends despise, forsake you?
    Take it to the Lord in prayer!
In His arms He'll take and shield you;
    You will find a solace there.

Blessed Savior, Thou hast promised
    Thou wilt all our burdens bear
May we ever, Lord, be bringing
    All to Thee in earnest prayer.
Soon in glory bright unclouded
    There will be no need for prayer
Rapture, praise and endless worship
    Will be our sweet portion there.

Mother Was a Lady

This seemingly imperishable ballad originated in the mid-1890s in a little basement saloon on 21st Street in New York. Edward Marks and Joseph Stern overheard two men teasing a new waitress, who finally burst into tears and said, "No one would dare to insult me if my brother Jack was only here," adding, "My mother was a lady." Marks, recognizing the possibilities of the line, immediately wrote the lyrics and Stern supplied the music. The song was sung with great success the next day at Tony Pastor's theatre. For those who might not know, a "drummer" was a traveling salesman. ❖

Mother Was a Lady

Words by Edward B. Marks
Music by Joseph W. Stern

Two drummers sat at dinner, in a grand hotel one day,
While dining they were chatting in a jolly sort of way,
And when a pretty waitress brought them a tray of food,
They spoke to her familiarly in manner rather rude;
At first she did not notice them, or make the least reply,
But one remark was passed that brought the teardrops to her eye,
And facing her tormentor, with cheeks now burning red,
She looked a perfect picture as appealingly she said:

Chorus:
"My mother was a lady, like yours, you will allow,
And you may have a sister, who needs protection now;
I've come to this great city to find a brother dear,
And you wouldn't dare insult me, Sir, if Jack were only here."

It's true one touch of nature, it makes the whole world kin,
And ev'ry word she uttered seemed to touch their hearts within.
They sat there stunned and silent, until one cried in shame,
"Forgive me, Miss! I meant no harm, pray tell me what's your name?"
She told him and he cried again, "I know your brother, too;
Why, we've been friends for many years and he often speaks of you.
He'll be so glad to see you, and if you'll only wed,
I'll take you to him as my wife, for I loved you since you said:"

Chorus:
"My mother was a lady, like yours, you will allow,
And you may have a sister, who needs protection now.
I've come to this great city to find a brother dear,
And you wouldn't dare insult me, Sir, if Jack were only here."

Mother

Words by Howard Johnson
Music by Theodore F. Morse

've been around the world, you bet,
ut never went to school;
ard knocks are all I seem to get;
erhaps I've been a fool;
ut still some educated folks,
upposed to be so swell,
Would fail if they were called upon,
simple world to spell.
low if you'd like to put me to a test,
here's one dear name that I can spell the best.

horus:
1 is for the million things she gave me,
) means only that she's growing old,
is for the tears she shed to save me,
1 is for her heart of purest gold,
is for her eyes with lovelight shining,
means right, and right she'll always be,
ut them all together, they spell MOTHER,
word that means the world to me.

When I was but a baby,
Long before I learned to walk,
While lying in my cradle,
I would try my best to talk.
It wasn't long before I spoke,
And all the neighbors heard—
My folks were very proud of me
For "mother" was the word.
Although I'll never lay a claim to fame,
I'm satisfied that I can spell the name.

Chorus:
M is for the mercy she possesses,
O means that I owe her all I own,
T is for her tender, sweet caresses,
H is for her hands that made a home,
E means everything she's done to help me,
R means real and regular, you see,
Put them all together, they spell MOTHER,
A word that means the world to me.

The Goodest Mother

vening was falling, cold and dark,
And people hurried along the way
As if they were longing soon to mark
heir own home candle's cheering ray.

Before me toiled in the whirling wind
A woman with bundles great and small,
And after her tugged, a step behind,
he Bundle she loved best of all.

A dear little roly-poly boy,
With rosy cheeks, and a jacket blue,
Laughing and chattering full of joy,
And here's what he said—I tell you true:

You're the goodest mother that ever was."
A voice as clear as the forest bird's;

And I'm sure the glad young heart had cause
To utter the sweet of the lovely words.

Perhaps the woman had worked all day
Washing or scrubbing; perhaps she sewed;
I knew, by her weary footfall's way,
That life for her was an uphill road.

But here was comfort, children dear.
Think what a comfort you might give,
To the very best friend you can have here,
The lady fair in whose house you live,

If once in a while you'd stop and say,
In task or play for a moment pause,
And tell in sweet and winning way,
"You're the *goodest* mother that ever was."

A Song From the
Old Country

By Mario DeMarco

O n occasion when the mood is right, my thoughts will wander back to the time when I was a mere youngster, happily residing with my family. My loving mother had her hands full in those Depression years—cooking, washing, sewing, housekeeping, chopping wood and taking care of us.

My father, who had worked in a large machine shop, ran a grinder that took the burrs and rough spots from pieces of steel that came out of a hot furnace. One day he was not protected from dustlike steel particles and inhaled some of them. They settled in his lungs, and in time his poor health forced him to quit. (Back then, protection was not a safety issue as it is today.) But even with all of my mother's daily tasks, she made sure that my father remained happy and comfortable.

Sometimes, when all her chores were done, she would sit in her favorite rocking chair and cuddle me on her lap, rocking and singing some of her favorite songs from "the old country," which was Naples, Italy. She sang softly with my head resting against her wide shoulders.

I loved each song she sang, but there was one in particular that had been a hit in Italy at the time. It was *O Sole Mio*. With that song, she had a unique way of calming any anxiety or depression I might have had at the time. It must have brought back pleasant memories for her, too, because when I looked at her beautiful, calm face, I would see that "far-away look" as she relived pleasant memories of her country with it abundant sunshine. She sang a variety of songs, but *O Sole Mio* became my favorite.

> *Sometimes, when all her chores were done, she would sit in her favorite rocking chair and cuddle me on her lap, rocking and singing some of her favorite songs from "the old country," which was Naples, Italy.*

During World War II, when I was serving in the Armed Forces, I was sent overseas to help reinforce U.S. Army troops that had suffered a setback after a surprise move by the enemy. The combat engineers had worked their men to the Rhine River and had captured a strategic bridge, intact. It had been a devastating and deadly battle before we were able to capture it. Our company had taken over one of the homes along the river, and had taken time out to rest and maintain the bridge.

While at that house, I came across a stack of records packed next to a hand-cranked Victrola. Looking through the pile, I was shocked and delighted to find one entitled *O Sole Mio* that was recorded in German!

put it on the Victrola and listened as the wonderful, familiar melody transported me back to my early childhood years. For those few precious moments, I was back home, and the sounds of war and the terrible destruction of this once beautiful countryside were forgotten.

I carried that record in my pack for several weeks, playing it whenever I had the opportunity. One day, when we were ordered to a specific area, our column was suddenly attacked by enemy planes. I was carrying a full pack and quickly dove into a shallow slit trench on the side of the road. When the action was over, I checked my pack, and to my dismay, the record had been broken. I tried to find another, but I never succeeded. It seemed that the record I had found was a rare one, and only a few were available.

After my time in the service, I was discharged and returned home. My mother was a bit older, but her features were still beautiful. My father had died, but still she carried on with her daily tasks. And in the evening, when all her chores were done, she still sat in her rocking chair, singing her favorite Italian songs, including *O Sole Mio*. It was a pleasant sight to see, and I was happy listening to her sing. I was grateful to see this sight again, as were my brothers, all of whom had returned safely from the devastating war. My mother passed away a short time later.

Several years later I purchased a Dean Martin album of Italian songs. One song in particular was outstanding—*O Sole Mio*. When I played this song, the memories rushed back and brought calm to me once again. ❖

O Sole Mio

Che bella cosa è na iurnata 'e sole
N'aria serena doppo na tempesta!
Pe' ll'aria fresca pare già na festa …
Che bella cosa na jurnata 'e sole

When I first saw you with your smile so tender,
My heart was captured, my soul surrendered.
I spent a lifetime waiting for the right time
Now that you're near, the time is here at last!

Chorus:
Ma n'aut sole chiù bello oi nè
O sole mio sta 'nfronte a te!
O sole o sole mio
Sta 'nfronte a te
Sta 'nfronte a te.

It's now or never, come hold me tight,
Kiss me, my darling, be mine tonight.
Tomorrow will be too late
It's now or never—
My love won't wait.

Quanno fa notte e 'o sole se ne scenne
Me vene quase' na malincunia
Sotto a fenesta toia restarria
Quanno fa notte e 'o sole se ne scenne

© *Special Moment With Mother* by Mario DeMarco

Just like a willow we would cry an ocean
If we lost true love and sweet devotion.
Your lips excite me, let your arms invite me,
For who knows when we'll meet again this way.

Love & the Power Of Music

By Ross Princiotto

I considered a night lost as a teenager during my senior year at Washington High School in Massillon, Ohio, whenever I did not play my favorite ballads on the Philco radio/record player. It had been a birthday gift to me from Mama.

As I played the records, Mama was always close by in the kitchen, darning my socks, ironing my trousers or crocheting doilies, and humming the tunes as I silently sang the words.

Mama was Sicilian and was not fluent in English, but she understood the spoken word of the songs. Mama and I shared quality time in the early hours of the evening, when she and I were alone. Warmth permeated the air in my home on Geiger Avenue Southwest, in the neighborhood called Little Europe. Nostalgia reigned, and even now in the December of my years, I reminisce about those Good Old Days.

Of course, Mama appreciated the vintage Italian records of Enrico Caruso she and Dad had brought over from Sicily. We often hear the standards on television even now: *O Sole Mio, Marie* and *Funiculi, Funnicula.* I wondered what fantasies Mama conjured as she listened to the Italian songs as well as the American ballads.

It was wartime in the 1940s—a time for patriotic songs, but mostly love songs and ballads. Although Bing Crosby, the Andrews Sisters and Dinah Shore were heard most often on the radio, the Mills Brothers, with their inimitable style, matched by no other vocalists of the day, were Mama's favorites and mine was well. We connected!

Do you remember *Paper Doll, You Always Hurt the One You Love, Poor Butterfly, Taxi* or *Till Then?* These standards were played often during the war years. Mama's favorite was *Till Then.*

I found out that during my two years in the U.S. Army in the South Pacific, my brothers and sisters were forbidden to play *Till Then.* They understood; the song reminded Mama of a superior time with her teenage son "Risario," as she used to call me. While I was in basic training at Camp Wolters, Texas, and in the Philippines and Japan, I grew misty-eyed as I enjoyed many times the songs I had shared with Mama.

In those Good Old Days, my favorite song by the Mills Brothers was *You Always Hurt the One You Love,* with words and music by Allan Roberts and Doris Fisher:

You Always Hurt the One You Love

You always hurt the one you love
The one you shouldn't hurt at all
You always take the sweetest rose
And crush it till the petals fall

You always break the kindest heart
With a hasty word you can't recall
So if I broke your heart last night,
It's because I love you most of all

Ti amo bene, Mama … grazie! I love you very much, Mama … thanks! ❖

Danny Boy

By James T. Page Jr.

Danny Boy was written by an English barrister from a sheet of music sent to him by his sister-in-law who said it was the tune *Londonderry Air* and had no lyrics. Frederic Weatherly used the words from a poem he wrote, and the words fit the music. *Danny Boy* is still referred to as *Londonderry Air*, but for me, it will always be my mother's song. Even now, at 83, when I hear *Danny Boy*, I think of her.

Mary Carr was the youngest (and, I've been told, the prettiest) daughter of an Irish immigrant family of eight boys and four girls. She was headstrong, spoiled and charming. She was also my mother.

From my toddler days in the 1920s, I remember her singing or humming, "Danny boy, the pipes, the pipes are calling." In reality, her voice left something to be desired, but to her young son, it was beautiful.

This American-born Irish lass married James Page when he returned from serving in World War I in France. They settled in Maplewood, Mo., a suburb of St. Louis, where she had been born and raised. When I came along, she wanted to name me Daniel. Family pressure, however, persuaded her to name me after my father, and so I became James Jr.

Like millions of Americans in the 1930s, we were victims of the Depression. But even though times were tough, my mother somehow managed to spend 39 cents on a record of *Danny Boy*. We played that record until the music turned into static, and we still listened.

But why *Danny Boy*? Perhaps she loved the Irish nature of the song, or maybe the soft lyrics and soothing melody. Whatever it was, she often said that she would love to have *Danny Boy* sung at her funeral. She passed away in 1984 in a convalescent home in St. James, Mo. I went back to handle the funeral, and I tried to find someone who could sing *Danny Boy*. But St. James is a small town and I could find no one to sing it. So instead, when I gave the eulogy, I read the lyrics of her favorite song. ❖

Danny Boy

O Danny Boy, the pipes, the pipes are calling
From glen to glen,
    and down the mountain side.
The summer's gone, and all the roses falling;
'Tis you, 'tis you must go and I must bide.

But come ye back
    when summer's in the meadow,
Or when the valley's hushed
    and white with snow
'Tis I'll be there in sunshine or in shadow;
Oh Danny Boy, oh Danny Boy, I love you so!

And if you come,
    and all the flow'rs are dying
And I am dead, as dead I well may be,
You'll come and find
    the place where I am lying
And kneel and say an "Ave" there for me.

And I shall hear,
    tho' soft you tread above me;
And all my dreams will warmer, sweeter be
If you'll not fail to tell me that you love me
I simply sleep in peace until you come to me.

My Mother's Voice

By Warren Dowling

I was raised in Oklahoma on a cotton farm where I was the ninth of 10 children. Needless to say, my mother was a very busy person and didn't have much time to give attention to each of us. One way she could entertain us was by singing the songs of that period. After the work for the day was over and we gathered around the fire, someone would say, "Mom, why don't you sing us some songs?" Sometimes she would be too tired to sing, but most times she would sing to us.

It has been so long ago that I don't remember if she had a good voice or not. I just remember that all of us kids enjoyed hearing her sing. She had about a half-dozen songs that she sang from memory. I heard them so much that after a while, I could identify with the characters.

This song is the one I remember best. As she sang about the different people, I imagined I could see them all, acting out their parts. Seventy-five years later, I can still follow the action as I read the song *The Lightning Express*. ❖

The Lightning Express

The Lightning Express from a depot so grand
Was just starting out on its way,
And all of the passengers who were on board
Seemed to be happy and gay,
Except a small boy in a seat by himself,
Who was reading a letter he had;
It was plain to be seen by the tears in his eyes
That the contents of it made him sad.

A stern old conductor then came through the car,
Taking tickets from everyone there,
And finally reaching the side of the boy,
He roughly demanded his fare.

"I have not a ticket," the boy did reply,
"But I'll pay you back some day."
"I'll have to put you off at the station," he said,
But he stopped as he heard the boy say,

Chorus:
"Oh, please Mister Conductor,
Don't put me off of your train,
For the best friend I have in the world
Is waiting for me in pain,
Is expected to die any moment,
And may not live through the day;
I want to see Mother and bid her goodbye
Before God takes her away."

A little girl sitting in a seat by herself
Said, "Don't put him off, it's a shame."
And taking his hat a collection she made
And soon paid his fare on the train.
"I am obliged to you, Miss, for your kindness."
"To me you're welcome, I'm sure I don't care."
Every time the conductor would come through the car,
These words seemed to ring in his ear:

Chorus:
"Oh, please Mister Conductor,
Don't put me off of your train,
For the best friend I have in the world
Is waiting for me in pain,
Is expected to die any moment,
And may not live through the day;
I want to see Mother and bid her goodbye
Before God takes her away."

Hello Central, Give Me Heaven

"Papa, I'm so sad and lonely,"
Sobbed a tearful little child,
"Since dear Mama's gone to Heaven
Papa, darling, you'll not smile.
I will speak to her and tell her
That we want her to come home,
You must listen and I'll call her,
On the telephone."

Chorus:
"Hello, Central, give me Heaven
For my Mama's there;
You will find her with the angels
On the golden stair;
Don't you tell her,
*   it's me who's speaking?*
Call her, won't you please;
For I want to surely tell her,
We're so lonely here?"

When the girl received the message
Coming through the telephone,
How her heart beat at the moment,
And the wires seemed to moan;
"I will tell you that I've found her,
Yes, dear heart, I'm coming home."
"Kiss me, Mama, kiss your darling,
Through the telephone."

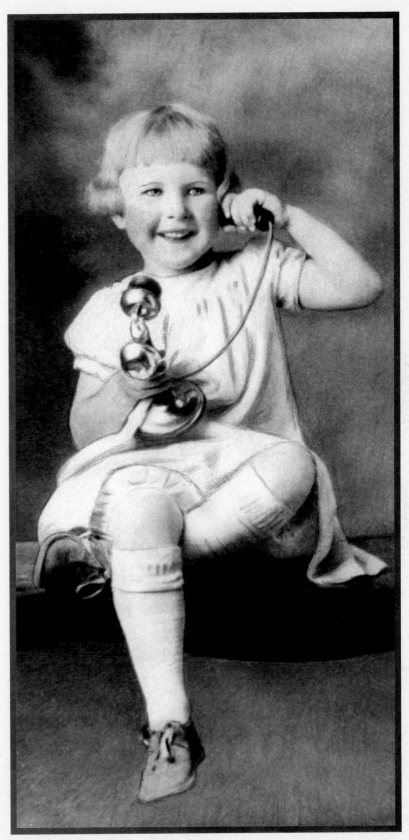

Hi Sweetie!, House of White Birches nostalgia archives

Old Folks at Home

Words and music by Stephen C. Foster

*I*n *Old Folks at Home*, the official song of Florida, Stephen Foster writes about the Suwannee ("Swanee") River, which flows south from the Okefenokee Swamp in Georgia to the Gulf of Mexico in Florida.

Below are the more modern words to this old popular folk song. The original chorus included a reference to "darkeys." We have used "dear ones" in replacement, following the suggestion of Leon and Lynn Dallin in *Heritage Songster*. In 1978, when the new Florida Capitol was dedicated, the program included the words to the State Song. Then "brothers" was the substituted word in the chorus. ❖

Old Folks at Home

Way down upon the Swanee River,
Far, far away
That's where my heart is turning ever
That's where the old folks stay
All up and down the whole creation,
Sadly I roam
Still longing for the old plantation
And for the old folks at home

Chorus:
All the world is sad and dreary,
Everywhere I roam
Oh dear ones, how my heart grows weary
Far from the old folks at home

All 'round the little farm I wandered,
When I was young'
Then many happy days I squandered,
Many the songs I sung …
When I was playing with my brother,
Happy was I …
Oh, take me to my kind old mother,
There let me live and die

One little hut among the bushes,
One that I love
Still sadly to my mem'ry rushes,
No matter where I rove
When shall I see the bees a humming,
All 'round the comb
When shall I hear the banjo strumming,
Down by my good old home

The Story of a Song

By Liza Janes

The song *The Picture Turned Toward the Wall* was inspired by a stage production *Blue Jeans*, a famous old melodrama by Joseph Arthur. The plot followed a proven audience pleaser: transgressing daughters turned out into a blizzard. Girls who courted their fathers' displeasure by leaving home to marry the man of their choice, or facing a fate worse than death by misalliance, were forbidden to ever darken the doors of their homesteads again, or have their names mentioned therein.

A struggling English songwriter, Charles Graham, who hadn't quite found the knack of pleasing the American public, happened to attend this tearjerker while it was enjoying a prosperous run at the 14th Street Theatre in New York City. While he realized it was an era wallowing in sentiment and pathos, he hadn't yet hit the mark. However, when Charles saw the irate father onstage violently turn his offspring's picture toward the wall, inspiration sadly smiled upon him and he returned home and wrote the lyrics for *The Picture Turned Toward the Wall*.

With emotion, sadness and sorrow now put to words, it remained for him to devise the music. He had access to the piano at the music publishing offices of M. Witmark and Sons, so he took himself there to explore a melody.

When the manuscript was completed, he showed it to young Julius P. Witmark, a member of the firm who was known from coast to coast as "the boy tenor." Julius was intrigued by the ballad and not only prevailed upon his partners to publish it, but included it as a song in a new musical then in preparation: *The City Directory*, which was to open soon at the Bijou Threatre.

The night the show opened and Julius stood on the stage and sang *The Picture Turned Toward the Wall*, there were few dry eyes in the audience, ensuring triumph for both the song and the young tenor. This success was repeated throughout the country and the ballad became one of the best-selling songs in years.

Although Charles Graham wrote a sequel, *Her Father Has Turned the Dear Picture Back Again*, it never became as popular as its predecessor—which goes to prove that while forgiveness is an admirable and noble emotion, sin and renunciation are what sell books, plays and songs. ❖

The Picture Turned Toward the Wall

Words and music by Charles Graham

Far away beyond the glamour
   of the city and its strife,
There's a quiet little homestead by the sea,
Where a tender, loving lassie
   used to live a happy life
Contented in her home as she could be;
Not a shadow ever seemed to cloud
   the sunshine of her youth,
And they tho't no sorrow could her life befall.
But she left them all one evening
   and their sad hearts knew the truth
When her father turned her picture
   toward the wall.

Chorus:
There's a name that's never spoken
   and a mother's heart half-broken,
Just another face that's missing
from the old home, that is all.
There is still a mem'ry living,
   there's a father unforgiving,
And a picture that is turned toward the wall.

They have laid away each token
   of the one who ne'er returns,
Ev'ry trinket, ev'ry ribbon that she wore,
Tho' it seems so long ago now,
   yet the lamp of hope still burns
And her mother prays to see her child once more
Tho' no tidings ever reach them
   what her life or lot may be,
Tho' they sometimes think she's gone
   beyond recall,
There's a tender recollection
   of a face they never see
In the picture that is turned toward the wall.

The Vacant Chair

Words by N.S.W.
Music by George F. Root

We shall meet, but we shall miss him,
There will be one vacant chair.
We shall linger to caress him,
When we breathe our evening prayer.
When a year ago we gathered,
Joy was in his mild blue eye,
But a golden cord is severed,
And our hopes in ruin lie.

Chorus:
We shall meet, but we shall miss him,
There will be one vacant chair;
We shall linger to caress him,
When we breathe our evening prayer.

At our fireside, sad and lonely,
Often will the bosom swell
At remembrance of the story
How our noble Willie fell;
How he strove to bear our banner
Thro' the thickest of the fight,
And uphold our country's honor,
In the strength of manhood's might.

True, they tell us wreaths of glory
Evermore will deck his brow,
But this soothes the anguish only
Sweeping o'er our heartstrings now.
Sleep today, O early fallen,
In thy green and narrow bed,
Dirges from the pine and cypress
Mingle with the tears we shed.

Do They Think of Me At Home?

Words by J.E. Carpenter
Music by Charles W. Glover

Do they think of me at home,
Do they ever think of me?
I who shared their ev'ry grief,
I who mingled in their glee?
Have their hearts grown cold and strange
To the one now doomed to roam?
I would give the world to know,
Do they think of me at home?
I would give the world to know,
Do they think of me at home?

Do they think of me at eve,
Of the songs I used to sing?
Is the harp I struck untouched,
Does a stranger wake the string?
Will no kind, forgiving word
Come across the raging foam?
Shall I never cease to sigh,
"Do they think of me at home?"
Shall I never cease to sigh,
"Do they think of me at home?"

Do they think of how I loved
In my happy, early days?
Do they think of him who came
But could never win their praise?
I am happy by his side,
And from mine he'll never roam,
But my heart will sadly ask,
"Do they think of me at home?"
But my heart will sadly ask,
"Do they think of me at home?"

Love of Country

Chapter Seven

ack in World War II, everyone knew the meaning of stars. For every person serving our country, a silver star gleamed in the window of that person's home.

Then there were gold stars.

Gold stars were usually preceded by the dreaded telegram: "We regret to inform you … ." Sometimes the telegram was accompanied by a military chaplain or a minister, but however the message came its message hit like a sledge-hammer. Some loved one had given the supreme sacrifice in the cause of freedom.

So a gold star replaced the silver star in the window. In close-knit communities, we all knew when tragedy struck one of our own, but the gold star gleamed so even strangers would know the mixed emotions of pride and grief that filled the home behind the window.

The first time I heard Tex Ritter sing *There's a Gold Star in Her Window*, I was struck with the pain a mother must feel upon the death of a son or daughter, no matter how noble the cause. Yet the song also conveyed the unmistakable love of country—a love so obviously passed from parent to child. A love the young man carried with him onto the field of battle. A love he held firmly to his last breath of life.

Songs of patriotism still move me to tears today. I remember in the days following the horror of Sept. 11, 2001, joining with fellow Americans in singing *God Bless America*. I remember my heart in my throat as we sang *The Star-Spangled Banner*. I remember watching as a new generation of Americans left for foreign frontiers in a new fight for freedom. And, again there would be mothers and fathers, sisters and brothers, wives, husbands and children swallowed up in pride and grief.

I don't think we put gold stars in windows any more.

Perhaps we should.

*There's a Gold Star
In Her Window*

**Words and Music by Tex Ritter
and Frank Harford**

There's a little gray-haired lady
You know as well as I.
Her eyes are always smiling
When yours and mine would cry.
Tho' she seems almost happy,
Her thoughts are far away;
She knows her boy is waiting
Where she will go someday.

There's a gold star in her window,
Shining bright and clear for all the world to see,
There's a gold star in her window,
Of the part a mother plays to keep us free.
To aid the cause of Liberty
She proudly gave a son,
Without the deeds of men like he,
No war is ever won.
There's a gold star in her window,
For a lad who led the way to victory.
There's a gold star in her window,
Shining bright and clear for all the world to see,
There's a gold star in her window,
Of the part a mother plays to keep us free.
'Twill shine throughout eternity
To guide us on our way,
Lest we forget or fail to see
The part we have to play;
There's a gold star in her window,
For a lad who led the way to victory.

—*Ken Tate*

It's a Grand Old Flag

I think it was my grandmother's father who, many, many years ago, escaped being drafted into the Kaiser's army—or so family lore has it. Instead, he came here to America and settled in New York state. He loved his adopted country as only an immigrant could. My grandmother, his daughter, was just as patriotic. However, it was my mother who would outdo them both.

I remember her singing or humming as she did her housework. She was not the best singer in the world, and she was not always—in fact not most of the time—in tune. But she made up for her lack of musical talent with the enthusiasm she put into every song. Mom had an amazing repertoire of songs that she would sing at the drop of a hat. Her sisters often joked that most of the time you didn't even have to drop a hat to get her started.

She knew just about every song Bing Crosby ever sang, and all the old tunes that my Grannie had taught her over the years, which were sad and always made me cry. One was *The Letter Edged in Black;* another was about someone tying up leaves because a person was going to die when the leaves fell from the trees. *Rock of Ages* and *The Old Rugged Cross* were also favorites.

Victory Garden by John Slobodnik, House of White Birches nostalgia archives

However, the tunes that really got her belting out the music were patriotic songs. And of all those, the first one that springs to mind when I think of Mom was *It's a Grand Old Flag*.

How she loved our flag and that song! No national holiday was a success for her unless that was played, and she always sang along. If we happened to be outside and passed a flag, immediately Mom would start humming, and soon I was humming along with her. During World War II, when Mom saw a flag waving, she would remark that it was flying in honor of my dad who was overseas in Europe. Sometimes Mom would say that it was there for Uncle Bill in the Pacific, or Uncle Joe or Uncle Ray in the Navy.

She often declared that she believed our flag was the most beautiful in all the world, and that was why it was called Old Glory, and we should feel pride in our Star-Spangled Banner. Mom would explain the meaning of the stars for our states and the red and white stripes for the 13 original colonies. On national holidays, Mom always dressed in red, white and blue.

Mom recalled her grandfather telling her how wonderful this country was and how lucky he was to be here. He told her that she should be proud to be an American, and she was. She could recite from memory many poems like *In Flanders Field* or *Paul Revere's Ride* or *America for Me* by Henry Van Dyke. But it was her singing *It's a Grand Old Flag* that we heard most often; it was her very special favorite and mine, too.

One of her most beloved poems was *The Flag Goes By* by Henry Holcomb Bennett. I can almost hear her voice reciting with conviction:

The Flag Goes By

Hats off!
Along the streets here comes
A blare of bugles, a ruffle of drums,
A flash of color beneath the sky,
Hats off!
The flag is passing by!

It was not just our flag, she would assert; it was what it represented. She believed that it honored each and every serviceman who had fallen beneath its colors as well as the ones who returned home after the horrible fighting. The flag deserved our respect. Mom knew that it should never touch the ground or be thrown away in the trash, but be burned instead when it grew old, faded or tattered.

There has not been a Fourth of July or Veterans Day since Mom's passing that I have not closed my eyes and seen her wearing her red, white and blue, and heard her voice inside my head, singing (still off-key, perhaps) *It's a Grand Old Flag*. After all these years, I can still recall those words to the chorus as if it were just yesterday and Mom beside me, singing:

It's a Grand Old Flag

It's a grand old flag,
It's a high-flying flag
And forever in peace may it wave.
It's the emblem of the land I love,
The home of the free and the brave!
Every heart beats true
For the red, white and blue,
And there's never a boast or a brag.
Should old acquaintance be forgot,
Keep your eye on that grand old flag!

Henry James once said that patriotism is like charity: It begins at home. I was taught well, and always have a flag flying in front of my home. If Mom were here now, I would tell her that it still is a grand old flag, and God willing, it always will be. ❖

Three Cheers for the Red, White & Blue

My song is actually a variation of Columbia, the Gem of the Ocean.
It was popular in our Philadelphia grade school during World War II.

By Dorothy Stanaitis

Finishing Touches to Old Glory by John Slobodnik, House of White Birches nostalgia archives

We asked our little grandson if he knew why flags were flying up and down the street on June 14. "Is it because the big kids are getting out of school for the summer?" he ventured.

Evidently he hadn't heard much about Flag Day at nursery school. I was surprised, because in my Philadelphia childhood, Flag Day was one of the year's highlights.

We all knew that a Philadelphia lady had made the first flag, and some of us even had visited her home—a tiny brick house near the Delaware River. Betsy Ross had her upholstery shop there, and it was in that house that Gen. George Washington had asked Betsy to sew

America's first flag, the Stars and Stripes.

At James Rhodes Elementary, we celebrated Flag Day outdoors. The classes would march onto the playground, which was surrounded by a tall wrought-iron fence. Parents and friends from the community would stand on the sidewalk outside the fence during the program. Our mother, pushing a carriage bearing our little brother, Charles, came each year to watch me and my little sister perform.

The program was usually the same: a number of patriotic songs, a few poems and, of course, the highlight of the day, the flag salute.

Patriotic fervor had grown intensely during World War II, and the group of adults gathered around the wrought-iron fence had grown larger also.

We were wild with excitement the year we had two new surprises for the Flag Day celebration. We had learned the flag salute in kindergarten, and now it was being changed. We had always said, "I pledge allegiance to the flag," and at the word *flag*, we thrust our arm forward. But since we were now at war with Germany, that arm thrust was too much like the gesture used with the words, "Heil, Hitler." This year, we would hold our right hands to our hearts and there would be no arm thrusts.

The second surprise was a new song. Well, it really wasn't new; the melody and the original words were familiar to everyone. But in honor of Flag Day, new words had been added to the song *Columbia the Gem of the Ocean*.

At last, the big day came. Most of the girls in my class wore new red, white or blue ribbons in

eir hair. Some of us were dressed in patriotic
olors, but all of us were nervous as we lined up
 march onto the playground. There was such a
arge group of parents watching us. And would we
ll remember the new words to our special song?

We were lined up according to size, the
irls in one line and the boys in another. It was
me to head out of the classroom and begin
ne program.

The sun was shining. The day was warm, but
 light breeze was blowing, just enough to float
ne flag. The kindergarten classes began by sing-
ng. I could see my mother at the fence. She blew
ne a kiss. I grinned at her, but kept my arms at
ny side as we had been instructed by the teacher.

Each class performed its songs and poems.
here was so much applause that it heartened
ne performers and gave them encouragement
 sing with even more gusto than usual. Then
ne program drew to the finale as the fifth grade
nished their part of the performance. Soon it
vould be time for the entire school to join to
ing our Flag Day song and try the new salute.
he teacher gave the signal by blowing on her
itch pipe and we caroled out to the tune of
Columbia the Gem of the Ocean.

Betsy Ross lived on Arch Street near Second.
Her sewing was very, very fine.
George Washington came down to see her,
To order in a brand-new flag.
Six white stripes and seven pretty red ones,
Thirteen stars upon a field of blue,
Twas the first flag our country ever floated,
Three cheers for the red, white and blue.

Three cheers for the red, white and blue.
Three cheers for the red, white and blue.
Twas the first flag our country ever floated,
Three cheers for the red, white and blue.

Our parents' applause was tumultuous. They
oved the new song. We glowed with pride.

The applause had barely faded when a sixth-
rade boy went to the flagpole to lead the flag
alute. We placed our right hands firmly over
ur hearts and held them there. Our voices rang
ut loud and clear: "I pledge allegiance to the
ag." As we recited the pledge, the words of our
new song echoed in my ears. "Three cheers for
the red, white and blue. Three cheers for the red,
white and blue." ❖

Editor's note: *There are several versions of the third
verse of* Columbia the Gem of the Ocean. *We have
chosen one of the most popular as a representative.*

Columbia the Gem Of the Ocean

Words and music by David T. Shaw, 1843

O Columbia! the gem of the ocean,
The home of the brave and the free,
The shrine of each patriot's devotion,
A world offers homage to thee.
Thy mandates make heroes assemble
When liberty's form stands in view;
The banners make tyranny tremble
When borne by the Red, White and Blue,
When borne by the Red, White and Blue,
The banners make tyranny tremble
When borne by the Red, White and Blue.

When war winged its wide desolation,
And threatened the land to deform,
The ark then of freedom's foundation,
Columbia, rode safe through the storm:
With her garlands of vict'ry around her,
When so proudly she bore her brave crew,
With her flag proudly floating before her,
The boast of the Red, White and Blue,
The boast of the Red, White and Blue,
With her flag proudly floating before her,
The boast of the Red, White and Blue.

"Old Glory" to greet, now come hither,
With eyes full of love to the brim,
May the wreaths of the heroes ne'er wither,
Nor a star of our banner grow dim;
May the service, united, ne'er sever,
But they to their colors prove true;
The Army and Navy forever,
Three cheers for the Red, White and Blue,
Three cheers for the Red, White and Blue,
The Army and Navy forever,
Three cheers for the Red, White and Blue!

A Beloved Anthem

By Roy Meador

The passing of songwriter Irving Berlin in 1989 ended an amazing era and career.

The poor immigrant boy who told America's story in song and gave his adopted country *God Bless America, White Christmas* and *Easter Parade* was born Israel Baline in Siberia on May 11, 1888. He arrived in New York more than a century ago in 1893 with his family, after their home was destroyed by Russian Cossacks.

Berlin's was truly a rags-to-riches Horatio Alger story, thanks to his hard work and gift for happy tunes people remembered.

From destitute newsboy and street singer for coins, he progressed to a job as a singing waiter in a New York Chinatown slum. Soon after that, he moved to Tin Pan Alley as a songwriter.

He began creating the songs America sings starting in 1907 with this first hit, *Marie From Sunny Italy*. Today America still eagerly sings and cherishes perpetual hits from the seemingly bottomless Berlin song bag.

Among those immortal melodies are *Say It With Music, Alexander's Ragtime Band, Always, Blue Skies* and *Let Me Sing and I'm Happy*. Berlin's 1942 classic, *White Christmas*, which Bing Crosby sang in the film *Holiday Inn*, has often been called America's most popular song.

In addition to his tender ballads of love and sentiment and other songs to lift the spirit, Berlin also composed a patriotic hit often recommended as an alternate national anthem to **The Star-Spangled Banner** *and much easier to sing—* **God Bless America.**

In addition to his tender ballads of love and sentiment and other songs to lift the spirit, Berlin also composed a patriotic hit often recommended as an alternate national anthem to *The Star-Spangled Banner* and much easier to sing—*God Bless America.*

Berlin originally wrote *God Bless America* in 1918 for the World War I Army show *Yip, Yip, Yaphank*. The show opened in New York on Aug. 19, 1918. Act 2 featured Pvt. Irving Berlin in person, singing the famous soldier's lament, *Oh, How I Hate to Get Up in the Morning*.

But Berlin and the show's producers decided against using *God Bless America* in the Army show, instead substituting the song *We're on Our Way to France*.

God Bless America went unused into his song bag and stayed there for 20 years.

Then, in 1938, singer Kate Smith asked Berlin to supply a new song for her Armistice Day radio show. She wanted a song to rally American nd remind them of their heritage at a time when var clouds again threatened world peace.

Berlin considered writing a new song. Then e recalled the 1918 words and melody he lready had waiting in the wings. He changed ne lyrics to make them appropriate for 1938, nd Kate Smith sang *God Bless America* for the rst time on her Nov. 10, 1938, radio program.

No other song in history earned such wift and widespread acclaim. Americans merging from the Great Depression and roubled about war overseas took the song o their hearts. Both major political parties dopted the song for the 1939 conventions. Kate Smith's recording was soon a smash uccess. The song was featured at public vents nationwide, including the presiden- ial birthday ball for President Franklin D. Roosevelt.

Irving Berlin, out of love for and loyalty to is adopted country, refused to profit personally rom the song's overwhelming acceptance. He et up a trust fund for the Boy and Girl Scouts of America, whereby all earnings from *God Bless America* go to those organizations permanently.

Irving Berlin was honored on Feb. 18, 1955, by the country he put so happily to music for most of his 100 years. President Dwight D. Eisenhower bestowed on him a gold medal authorized by an ct of Congress in recognition and appreciation of is "services in composing many popular songs, ncluding *God Bless America.*"

During his latter decades, when the idea requently was broached of making *God Bless America* the nation's official national anthem, Berlin opposed the idea. He didn't want his ong to undermine the long history behind *The Star-Spangled Banner*. The man known as "Mr. Show Business" was content to have is song remain an unofficial "understudy" o *The Star-Spangled Banner* and the popular hoice of millions of people who joined him n loving America.

In 1964, the American Society of Compos- rs, Authors and Publishers named 16 songs to ts All-Time Hit Parade. On the list were three by Irving Berlin: *Alexander's Ragtime Band*, *White Christmas* and *God Bless America*. ❖

God Bless America

Words and music by Irving Berlin

*While the storm clouds gather far across
    the sea,
Let us swear allegiance to a land that's free.
Let us all be grateful for a land so fair,
As we raise our voices in a solemn prayer:*

God, bless America,
Land that I love.
Stand beside her, and guide her,
Through the night with a light from above.
From the mountains, to the prairies,
To the oceans white with foam,
God, bless America,
My home, sweet, home.

American popular music composer Irving Berlin (1888–1989) plays a piano and sings into a microphone while recording a film score in his studio, Hollywood, Calif. Berlin, who composed many standards in the American Songbook, never learned to read music. Circa 1935
Hulton Archive/Getty Images

Music Under the Stars

By Angie Monnens

*M*ost people are familiar with gatherings in large fields to accommodate thousands watching and listening to their favorite musicians in live concerts, but the idea isn't new. I recall such concerts in the 1930s, when I was a young girl living in Cold Spring, Minn. Each week, the town band performed in the park down by the Sauk River, and everyone brought their families for a night of music and fun.

Later, the city fathers decided to build a large structure on Main Street where the band could hold their concerts. Since stores remained open until 9 p.m., they reasoned, parents coul shop while waiting for the concert to begin.

They hoped these weekly concerts would become a great asset to our town's economy. They built the platforr high enough so all could see the musicians who gave of their time and talents for our enjoyment.

Every week we kids awaited Saturday, when we'd get our baths, put on our newest dresses and shirts, and head uptown with Mama and Daddy. He dropped us off on Main Street and then went back to work in the store he owned. As we met our friends and cousins, we linked arms and headed down Main Street, lured by the tempting aroma of buttery popcorn, made fresh all night long. We had a nickel to buy a bottle of the soda pop that was manufactured in our loca brewery, and another nickel for the popcorn.

We pranced up and down the street as Mama did her shopping. Soon the church bells rang the 8 o'clock hour. It was time for the fun to begin. Rows and rows of benches had been set up on the street to give everyone a place to sit. With so much shuffling about, a cloud of dust rose in a huge ball. Once the dust settled, so did the crowd.

> *A sudden hush fell, mothers quieted crying babies and we kids waited with great anticipation as the band came marching toward us from the village hall. The bandleader led the way, and with all the presence of a dignitary, he climbed the six steps to the platform.*

A sudden hush fell, mothers quieted crying babies and we kids waited with great anticipation as the band came marching toward us from the village hall. The bandleader led the way, and with all the presence of a dignitary, he climbed the six

The Cold Spring band in the early 1900s in their "Sunday suits" with John Wocken (far right) as their leader. By the 1930s they had snappy uniforms and Paul Wocken was the bandleader.

steps to the platform. The musicians followed. Once they were seated, he raised his baton, tapped it lightly on the tin music stand before him and nodded to the band.

Suddenly the blare of trumpets pierced the air, playing the prelude to a series of John Philip Sousa marches such as *Under the Double Eagle* and *Stars and Stripes Forever*. The lively music matched the spirit of the audience. Children danced and jigged in the street, making sure not to get in the way of adults seated on benches.

It made the night so much more exciting to see the musicians in their dark uniforms with gold stripes and epaulets. As I watched closely, some of them blew into their horns so hard that their cheeks puffed up like a squirrel's as he enjoyed a feast of acorns. I wondered if I would ever master the clarinet someday like these musicians.

The hour passed too quickly. The band played the national anthem, and the concert was over for another week. Everyone hung around town for a while, visiting and laughing while they rounded up their children. Babies slept in their mothers' arms and little brothers tried hard to stay awake.

When Daddy had the store cleaned and ready for the Sunday morning customers, he packed the groceries in the trunk of the car. We said good night to all our friends and went home.

As always, I found it hard to fall asleep. The lively music, the noise of the crowd, the laughter and giggles of my friends continued to stir around in my brain. When I finally fell asleep, I dreamed I sat on that platform, playing a clarinet solo as the whole town cheered wildly. However, my wonderful moment was cut short when my sister, lying beside me, cried and screamed. She was having another nightmare. Thus my moment in the spotlight ended abruptly.

I did learn to play the clarinet in seventh grade and made it to second chair a year later. Meanwhile, the townspeople continue to enjoy the summer concerts. Storekeepers happily noticed that their business improved, as did their profits.

Today the park by the river is still there, but things have changed, and there is no gazebo anywhere to be seen. The only music is the blast of boom boxes held by kids riding their bikes or carried by people walking the trails near the outskirts of town.

Even the school bands, with all their trappings, don't play Sousa marches anymore. But I still have fond memories from my youth that shall always be a wonderful part of my life! There's something special about a Sousa march that makes one walk just a little prouder. ❖

The Other Side
Of the Fence

By Nicole Grün.

The song *This Land Is Your Land* by Woody Guthrie will always remind my of Mr. McAfee. He had the best swing set in the neighborhood, or at least I thought so. It was small and rusty and had been well used by his children and grandchildren.

His family had long since outgrown the swing by the time I discovered it. I took to climbing the fence that separated our back yard from his and using his swing instead of the brand-new one my father had bought for me. It was on that swing that I began to sing.

From the time I learned to talk, I loved singing—first, the songs I learned in school, and later, those my father taught me. Mr. McAfee's swing set was the ideal place to sing. The squeaky rise and fall of the swing created a rhythmic tone that matched my songs. It soon became my favorite pastime.

I never thought about whether the neighbors could hear me. I sang because I enjoyed it, although I never objected to an audience. Sometimes, in the late afternoons, when the sun was setting and the air was cooling, Mr. McAfee would come outside and sit at the small wooden

The night was balmy, as summer nights in Texas tend to be, and the air was thick with the sound of locusts. Expertly, I pumped the swing high into the air so that I could feel the breeze.

picnic table near the swing. He seldom spoke, and in the twilight, his aging features were hardly distinguishable among the shadows. On most nights he would just sit peacefully, and I would continue my songs. It was on an evening like this that he first made a request.

The night was balmy, as summer nights in Texas tend to be, and the air was thick with the sound of locusts. Someone had been barbecuing nearby and the smell lingered. Expertly, I pumped the swing high into the air so that I could feel the breeze between my bare toes.

I was just beginning a new song when Mr. McAffee came out to take his usual seat. After about an hour or so, he quietly spoke. "*This Land Is Your Land*," he said. His voice was soft and his words had taken me by surprise; I wasn't sure I had heard him correctly. He said again, this time more clearly, "Please sing *This Land Is Your Land*."

As a grin spread across my face, I sang the song with more enthusiasm than ever. From that night on, whenever Mr. McAfee appeared, I sang his favorite song. It was my favorite also; I never told him that, but I think he knew.

In addition to the best swing set in the neighborhood, Mr. McAfee also had the best tree house. Eleven rotting boards nailed to the side of an old oak tree led the way to a platform in the clouds.

"Your mother worries about you," my father would tell me. He built a "tree house" in our yard for me—a miniature house with two rooms, a roof and windows, only a foot off the ground. But it was a wasted effort, because nothing could keep me from the one next-door. It was from Mr. McAfee's tree house that I could view every rooftop, and suddenly the neighborhood had no secrets.

The tree house and swing set had seen better days. When nature and an 8-year-old got to together, they didn't have a chance. The swing's chains were rusty and worn with weather and age.

1934 Kelloggs ad, House of White Birches nostalgia archives

My hands and clothes were always stained with its chalky brown residue.

One day as I was swinging, a chain broke and I fell to the ground with a shock. After inspecting myself for blood and bruises, I ran to the house as quickly as my legs would take me. I flew in the back door with a loud bang, and ran through the halls until I found my father's arms. Tearfully I explained what had happened. "Please, Daddy, can we fix the swing?" I pleaded. He promised to make a trip to the hardware store and fix the chain the next week.

But the next afternoon when I climbed the fence and peeked over at the swing set, there were two brand-new shiny silver chains in place of the old ones. I scrambled over the top of the fence and jumped to the ground. The swing was fixed, and I spent the rest of the evening singing in celebration. My father had been at work all day; it was Mr. McAfee who had fixed the swing.

Over the next few years, the swing and the tree house were kept in good repair. The swing eventually saw a new coat of paint, and then another. Gradually, as the tree house steps rotted and crumbled, they were also replaced. Part of the platform collapsed one day; luckily I wasn't there when it happened. Mr. McAfee always seemed to anticipate problems and make repairs before I could hurt myself. It wasn't until I was older that I realized how difficult it must have been for a man of his age to do such work.

September of the year I turned 11 is one I'll never forget. Over the summer I had grown taller and lost some baby fat. The girls and boys in my class no longer hated each other, and I had my first boyfriend. I also discovered that the fifth grade brought longer school days, harder lessons and homework every night. It was also the September of Mr. McAfee's death.

My mother picked me up from school that day. In the car, I was chatting happily about the day's events. Mom was unusually quiet. Eventually she interrupted me. "Honey, I have some bad news. Mr. McAfee passed away this morning. His son found him—he died in his sleep. I'm very sorry."

I was speechless—it didn't seem possible. I tried to recall when I had last seen him. I didn't want to remember that it had been over a month. That evening I crept over the fence and into the next yard. I went to the swing and sat. I didn't swing that night, and there weren't any songs. My silence matched that of Mr. McAfee's old house.

I'm not sure how long I sat that night. Without a jacket, I was freezing, although the cold didn't hurt me as much as the other pain. I think it was very late when my father came for me with his flashlight. With one arm protectively around my shoulders, he carefully led me the long way, around the fence, back home.

A few days later I missed school for Mr. McAfee's funeral. As I sat with my family in the large church, I wondered at all the people who were there. Every seat was filled, and the casket was not visible beneath all the flowers amassed around it.

As friends and family rose and spoke, I began to see a side of Mr. McAfee that I had never known. I learned that he had taught science at a local college for many years before his retirement. I also learned that he had served in the Navy, loved to dance, and had enjoyed fishing in his younger years. These were things I had never stopped to consider.

I guess nothing would have been different if I had known him better. For me, all that had mattered was the gentle way he smiled when I sang for him.

Mr. McAfee was buried at a site near my house. The morning following his funeral, I woke very early and dressed. Outside the morning air was cool and crisp. The sun had just begun its climb and it seemed to be resting in the uppermost branches of distant oak trees. I had left my bicycle in the driveway and the seat was wet with dew from the night before. As I rode toward the funeral home, I remembered that I had left behind the flowers I meant to bring for his grave. But I realized when I got there that there were already more flowers than his gravesite could hold. I laid my bike up against a tree and knelt in the wet grass near the many blooming plants.

About an hour later, a crew of workers arrived and began to unload equipment nearby. I thought to myself, as I got up to leave, that if they had arrived any earlier, they would have heard me singing *This Land Is Your Land*. ❖

This Land Is Your Land

Words and music by Woody Guthrie

Chorus:
This land is your land, this land is my land,
From California, to the New York island,
From the redwood forest,
  to the gulf stream waters,
This land was made for you and me.

As I was walking a ribbon of highway,
I saw above me an endless skyway,
I saw below me a golden valley,
This land was made for you and me.

Chorus

I've roamed and rambled
  and I've followed my footsteps,
To the sparkling sands of her diamond deserts,
And all around me a voice was sounding:
"This land was made for you and me."

Chorus

The sun comes shining as I was strolling,
The wheat fields waving
  and the dust clouds rolling,
The fog was lifting, a voice come chanting,
"This land was made for you and me."

Chorus

As I was walkin'—I saw a sign there,
And that sign said—no trespassin'
But on the other side … it didn't say nothin'!
Now that side was made for you and me!

Chorus

In the squares of the city—in the shadow
  of the steeple,
Near the relief office—I see my people,
And some are grumblin'
  and some are wonderin',
If this land's still made for you and me.

Chorus

There's a Star-Spangled Banner Waving Somewhere

By Paul Roberts and Shelby Darnell

There's a Star-Spangled Banner waving
    somewhere
In a distant land so many miles away.
Only Uncle Sam's great heroes get to go there
Where I wish that I could also live some day.
I'd see Lincoln, Custer, Washington and Perry,
And Nathan Hale and Colin Kelly, too!
There's a Star-Spangled Banner waving
    somewhere,
Waving o'er the land of heroes brave and true.

In this war with its mad schemes of destruction
Of our country fair and our sweet liberty
By the mad dictators, leaders of corruption,
Can't the U.S. use a mountain boy like me?
God gave me the right to be a free American,
And for that precious right I'd gladly die.
There's a Star-Spangled Banner waving
    somewhere,
That is where I want to live when I die.

Though I realize I am crippled, that is true, sir!
Please don't judge my courage by my twisted leg.
Let me show my Uncle Sam what I can do, sir!
Let me help to bring the Axis down a peg.
If I do some great deed I'll be a hero,
And a hero brave is what I want to be.
There's a Star-Spangled Banner waving
    somewhere,
In that heaven there must be a place for me!

A Song of a Thousand Years

By Henry C. Work

Lift up your eyes, desponding free men!
Fling to the winds your needless fears!
He who unfurl'd your beauteous banner,
Says it shall wave a thousand years!

Chorus:
"A thousand years!" my own Columbia!
'Tis the glad day so long foretold!
'Tis the glad morn whose early twilight
Washington saw in times of old.

What if the clouds, one little moment,
Hide the blue sky where morn appears,
When the bright sun,
    that tints them crimson,
Rises to shine a thousand years?

Tell the great world these blessed tidings!
Yes, and be sure the bondman hears;
Tell the oppressed of ev'ry nation,
Jubilee lasts a thousand years!

America the Beautiful

© John Sloane

This marvelous anthem was the favorite song of count- less Americans in the Good Old Days. The original version of the song was penned by Katharine Lee Bates in 1893. Writing about her com- position of *America the Beautiful*, Mrs. Bates said: "One day some of the other teachers and I decided to go on a trip to 14,000-foot Pikes Peak [in the Rocky Mountains of Colorado]. Near the top we had to leave the wagon and go the rest of the way on mules. I was very tired. But when I saw the view, I felt great joy. All the wonder of America seemed displayed there, with the sealike expanse."

Music later composed by Silas G. Pratt gave America one of its most enduring anthems.

America the Beautiful

O beautiful for spacious skies,
For amber waves of grain,
For purple mountain majesties
Above the fruited plain!
America! America!
God shed His grace on thee,
And crown thy good with brotherhood
From sea to shining sea!

O beautiful for pilgrim feet,
Whose stern, impassioned stress
A thoroughfare of freedom beat
Across the wilderness!
America! America!
God mend thine every flaw,
Confirm thy soul in self-control,
Thy liberty in law!

O beautiful for heroes proved
In liberating strife,
Who more than self their country loved
And mercy more than life!
America! America!
May God thy gold refine
Till all success be nobleness
And every gain divine!

O beautiful for patriot dream
That sees beyond the years
Thine alabaster cities gleam
Undimmed by human tears!
America! America!
God shed His grace on thee
And crown thy good with brotherhood
From sea to shining sea!

The Star-Spangled Banner

Words by Francis Scott Key
Music by John Stafford Smith

Oh, say, can you see by the dawn's early light,
What so proudly we hailed at the twilight's last gleaming?
Whose broad strips and bright stars, through the perilous fight,
O'er the ramparts we watched, were so gallantly streaming?
And the rockets' red glare, the bombs bursting in air,
Gave proof through the night that our flag was still there.
Oh, say, does that star-spangled banner yet wave
O'er the land of the free and the home of the brave?

On the shore, dimly seen through the mists of the deep,
Where the foe's haughty host in dread silence reposes,
What is that which the breeze, o'er the towering steep,
As it fitfully blows, half conceals, half discloses?
Now it catches the gleam of the morning's first beam,
In full glory reflected now shines on the stream:
'Tis the star-spangled banner! Oh, long may it wave
O'er the land of the free and the home of the brave!

And where is that band who so vauntingly swore
That the havoc of war and the battle's confusion
A home and a country should leave us no more?
Their blood has washed out their foul footsteps' pollution.
No refuge could save the hireling and slave
From the terror of flight, or the gloom of the grave;
And the star-spangled banner in triumph doth wave
O'er the land of the free and the home of the brave.

Oh, thus be it ever, when freemen shall stand
Between their loved home and the war's desolation;
Blest with victory and peace, may the heav'n-rescued land
Praise the Pow'r that hath made and preserved us a nation!
Then conquer we must, when our cause it is just,
And this be our motto: "In God is our trust."
And the star-spangled banner in triumph shall wave
O'er the land of the free and the home of the brave.

Index

Song Titles

Song of a Thousand Years 155

Alexander's Ragtime Band 101

Alice Blue Gown 13

America the Beautiful 157

Beneath the Cross of Jesus 71

Blest Be the Tie That Binds 128

By the Light of the Silvery Moon 19

Cielito Lindo 125

Columbia the Gem of the Ocean 147

Danny Boy 135

Do They Think of Me at Home? 141

Down By the Old Mill Stream 51

Down in the Valley 29

Farther Along 69

Five Foot Two 97

God Bless America 149

God, Who Touches Earth With Beauty 110

God Will Take Care of You 119

Good Night, Sweetheart 113

Hello Central, Give Me Heaven 137

Here Comes Santa Claus 87

Hiawatha's Melody of Love 7

Home's Not Merely Four Square Walls 118

How Great Thou Art 57

I'll Take You Home Again, Kathleen 14

I'm Knee Deep in Daisies
(And Head Over Heels in Love) 50

I'm Tying the Leaves So They Won't Come Down 53

Imagination 33

Indian Love Call 41

In My Merry Oldsmobile 96

It's a Grand Old Flag 145

Let's Just Go Nuts at Christmas 89

Johnny Ver Beck 112

Let Me Call You Sweetheart 44

Life's Railway to Heaven 73

Lilli Marlene 47

Love's Old Sweet Song 51

Mairzy Doats 95

My Happiness 37

Mother 131

Mother Was a Lady 129

No Disappointment in Heaven 77

Peg O' My Heart 49

O Holy Night 66

Oh Johnny, Oh Johnny, Oh! 105

Old Folks at Home 139

O Sole Mio 133

Outside of You 104

Over the Garden Wall 11

Roll Out the Barrel 93

Red Wing 7

Red River Valley 23

Rock Me to Sleep in My Rocky Mountain Home 31

Route 66 109

Rudolph the Red-Nosed Reindeer 86

Seeing Nellie Home 122

She'll Be Coming Round the Mountain 99

Shenandoah 29

Side By Side 35

Silent Night, Holy Night 115

Silver Threads Among the Gold 121

Silver-Haired Daddy of Mine 123

Sonny Boy 28

Sunrise Serenade 10

Take Me Out to the Ball Game 84

The Animal Fair 91

The Church in the Wildwood 16

The Flag Goes By 145

The Girl I Left Behind Me 48

The Goodest Mother 131

The Hand That Rules the World 116

The Lightning Express 136

The Old Rugged Cross 61

The Picture Turned Toward the Wall 140

The Star-Spangled Banner 158

The Vacant Chair 141

The Western Home (Home on the Range) 27

There's a Gold Star in Her Window 143

There's a Star-Spangled Banner Waving Somewhere 155

This Land Is Your Land 154

This Little Light of Mine 64

Two Little Girls in Blue 45

Wait for the Wagon 95

What a Friend We Have in Jesus 128

When You Wish Upon a Star 12

When It's Springtime in the Rockies 22

When the Roll Is Called Up Yonder 63

When Your Old Wedding Ring Was New 55

Where We'll Never Grow Old 79

Yankee Rose 39

Yes! We Have No Bananas! 81

You Always Hurt the One You Love 134

You Made Me Love You 48

First Lines

An old man gazed on a photograph,............................ 45
And the song they sang was Hiawatha's melody,.......... 7
Be not dismayed whate'er betide,........................... 119
Beneath the cross of Jesus I fain would
take my stand,... 71
Betsy Ross lived on Arch Street near Second. 146
Blest be the tie that binds our hearts in
Christian love, ... 128
Che bella cosa è na iurnata 'e sole, ... 133
Climb upon my knee, Sonny Boy;
you are only three,.. 28
Darling, I am growing, growing old;...................... 121
De la sierra morena viene bajando viene bajando, ... 125
Do they think of me at home, ... 141
Down in the valley, the valley so low,..................... 29
Ev'ry time I see the golden sunset in the west,........... 31
Evening shadows make me blue,............................. 37
Evening was falling, cold and dark 131
Far away beyond the glamour of the city
and its strife, ... 140
From this valley they say you are going, ... 23
Gee, it's great to be absolutely free, ... 104
God, who touches earth with beauty, ... 110
Good mornin', good mornin', you sleepyhead, ... 10
Good night, sweetheart, ... 113
Hats off! Along the streets here comes,................... 145
Here comes Santa Claus! Here comes Santa Claus!.... 87
Home's not merely four square walls,...................... 118
I am dreaming, Dear, of you day by day, ... 44
I have heard of a land on the faraway strand, ... 79
I just got a funny letter from a pal who went away, ... 50
I just saw a maniac, maniac, maniac, ... 97
I know a ditty nutty as a fruitcake, ... 95
I once had a gown—it was almost new,.................... 13
I went to the animal fair, ... 91
I'll take you home again, Kathleen,......................... 14
I've been around the world, you bet,...................... 131
If you ever plan to motor west,............................. 109
Imagination is funny 33
In a vine-covered shack in the mountain,................. 123
In the sky the bright stars glittered, ... 122
It's a grand old flag, it's a high-flying flag,.............. 145
Life is like a mountain railroad,............................. 73
Lift up your eyes, desponding free men!.................. 155
Mother sang those old songs,................................ 18
Nelly Kelly loved baseball games 84
O beautiful for spacious skies,.............................. 157
O Columbia! The gem of the ocean, ... 147
O Danny Boy, the pipes, the pipes are calling, ... 135
O holy night! The stars are brightly shining, ... 66
O Lord my God, when I in awesome wonder,............. 57
Oh, ma honey, oh, ma honey, ... 101
Oh! I yust go nuts at Christmas!............................. 89

Oh, give me a home where the buffalo roam,............. 27
Oh, Johnny! Oh, Johnny!.................................... 105
Oh, my love stood under a walnut tree, ... 11
Oh, say can you see by the dawn's early light,.......... 158
Oh, Shenandoah, I long to hear you, ... 29
On a hill far away stood an old rugged cross,............. 61
Once in the dear dead days beyond recall,................. 51
"Papa, I'm so sad and lonely," 137
Peg o' my heart, I love you,.................................. 49
Place park, scene dark,.. 19
Playmates were they, girl and lad,.......................... 53
See that sun in the morning peeking over the hill, ... 35
She'll be coming 'round the mountain
when she comes.. 99
Silent night! Holy night! 115
Take me out to the ball game,............................... 84
Tempted and tried we're oft' made to wonder 69
The dames of France are fond and free,................... 48
The Lightning Express from a depot so grand,.......... 136
The twilight shadows deepen in the night, dear,.......... 22
There once lived an Indian maid, ... 7
There was a little Dutchman,................................ 112
There's a church in the valley by the wildwood, ... 16
There's a fruit store on our street........................... 81
There's a garden, what a garden, ... 93
There's a little gray-haired lady 143
There's a Star-Spangled Banner
waving somewhere.. 155
There's no disappointment in heaven,...................... 77
They say that man is mighty,................................ 117
This land is your land, this land is my land, ... 154
This little light of mine, yes,................................ 64
Two drummers sat at dinner,
in a grand hotel one day,..................................... 129
Underneath the lantern, by the barrack gate,............. 47
Way down upon the Swanee River,......................... 139
We shall meet, but we shall miss him, ... 141
We've seen roses grow almost ev'rywhere,................ 39
What a friend we have in Jesus, all our sins
and griefs to bear!.. 128
When I'm calling you-oo-oo-oo 41
When the trumpet of the Lord shall sound,................ 63
When you wish upon a star,.................................. 12
When your old wedding ring was new,..................... 55
While the storm clouds gather far across the sea,...... 149
Will you come with me, my Phillis dear, ... 95
You always hurt the one you love, ... 134
You know Dasher and Dancer and Prancer
and Vixen,.. 86
You made me love you, I didn't wanna do it,............. 48
You must know that my uncle is a farmer,................. 51
Young Johnnie Steele has an Oldsmobile. 96